English Sketches

Sketches from the English Teaching Theatre

elementary

1

Doug Case
Ken Wilson

Heinemann

Heinemann English Language Teaching
A division of Reed Educational and Professional Publishing Limited
Halley Court, Jordan Hill, Oxford OX2 8EJ

OXFORD MADRID FLORENCE ATHENS PRAGUE SÃO PAULO MEXICO CITY
CHICAGO PORTSMOUTH (NH) TOKYO SINGAPORE KUALA LUMPUR
MELBOURNE AUCKLAND JOHANNESBURG IBADAN GABORONE

ISBN 0 435 26394 3

Designed by Kevin McGeoghegan MCSD

Cover design by Keith Shaw at Threefold Design

Cover photograph by Chris Kelly, showing Garry Fox, Matthew Bates and Angela Marshall in the 'Doctor' sketch.

Permission to copy

Acknowledgements

As in the original edition of *Off-Stage!*, we would like to thank BBC English by Radio & Television for permission to reproduce the 'Ticket Inspector' sketch, which was originally written by Doug Case for the radio series *Let's Speak English* and then adapted for the ETT's stage show.

And, as in the original editions of both *Off-Stage!* and *Further Off-Stage!*, we would like to express our thanks to these people:

- to John Haycraft, for having the original idea for the ETT, and for constant support and encouragement ever since;
- to Jeremy Harrison and Piers Plowright, who first gave the ETT a style and identity;
- to all the members of the ETT, past and present, who have performed with us on our tours;
- to all the organizations who have helped us with our tours, particularly International House and the British Council;
- and, most of all, to all the teachers and students who have been our audiences, organizers and hosts, for their help, kindness, hospitality and enthusiasm.

Doug Case & Ken Wilson
April 1995

Printed in Great Britain by Thomson Litho Ltd, East Kilbride, Scotland
Bound by Hunter and Foulis, Edinburgh, Scotland
97 98 99 10 9 8 7 6 5 4 3

Contents

Teacher's introduction

Structural levels chart

Index of language areas

Sketches

er's introduction

...s 1 and 2 are a set of Teacher's
...ks at two levels: Elementary (Book 1),
...iate (Book 2). Each book contains
...ches, which can be used by secondary
...dents and adult learners, in class or in other
...such as English clubs and end-of-term
...An audio cassette or compact disc containing
...ings of the sketches accompanies each book.

...sketches in these Teacher's Resource Books
...mprise twenty-three of the sketches which first
...ppeared in *Off-Stage!* and *Further Off-Stage!*,
originally published by Heinemann in 1979 and 1984
respectively, together with nine new sketches. All the
sketches are taken from shows performed by the
English Teaching Theatre between 1974 and 1994.

The English Teaching Theatre

The English Teaching Theatre (ETT) is a theatre
company which produces stage shows for learners of
English all over the world. The shows consist of
sketches, songs and other activities, all involving a lot
of audience participation, and are designed to be
enjoyed by both teenagers and adults; the format
evolved from a style of teaching in which the use of
sketches, songs and role-playing is considered very
useful. ETT performances take place in schools, in
adult education centres and in many other settings,
such as teacher-training institutes, language schools
and theatres.

The ETT was originally the idea of John Haycraft, the
former Principal of International House, London, a
private language school with branches and affiliates all
over the world. In 1969, John said to one of his
teachers, Jeremy Harrison: 'Why don't we have a
theatre specially for students of English?'

From 1970 to 1972, the ETT idea was developed in a
series of summer season performances in London.
Then, in 1973, the British Council invited the group to
tour Germany, and the touring side of the ETT's
work began. Since then, the group has undertaken
over 170 tours, visiting more than 40 countries
around the world; these countries include most of
Western Europe, seven countries in Latin and South
America, seven in West Africa, four in the Middle
East, Uzbekistan and Japan.

The usefulness of sketches

John Haycraft's summary of the usefulness of the ETT
applies equally well to the use of sketches in general:
'It makes students aware that English is not just words,
structures and idioms, but that it is a lively, dramatic
and versatile means of communication. It emphasizes
too, that learning and teaching can and should be
pleasurable.'

Sketches can, of course, be used simply as
entertaining material for listening or reading. Above
all, however, they provide enjoyable *speaking*
practice, whether they are re-enacted by the students
with their scripts in their hands, used as a basis for
improvisation, or learnt for a more elaborate
performance. They require attention to stress,
intonation and overall clarity: if the 'audience' can't
hear the words clearly, they won't be able to
appreciate the jokes! Depending on the context in
which the sketches are being used, the 'audience' may
simply be other students in the class, or an actual
audience. Whatever the context, working on
sketches is a collaborative activity and can have
benefits for general student interaction as well as for
language practice.

Choosing sketches from
English Sketches 1 and 2

Above all, we hope that you will be choosing a sketch
to do with your students because you believe that
they will find it funny and enjoyable.

All the sketches in *English Sketches* 1 and 2 can be
used at a variety of levels. Even if a sketch is
designated as 'elementary', its humour can make it
enjoyable for intermediate or more advanced
students; conversely, even a sketch designated as
'intermediate' may be useable with elementary
students, because its situation is clear and accessible –
and once again because of the humour.

The language used in the sketches is controlled but
not artificial. As a reviewer of one of the original
books, *Off-Stage!*, remarked, to our great pleasure:
'The material covers a fairly standard progression of
structures and functions, but the sketches are not so
crammed with obvious and repeated grammar points

as to be in any way tedious. Quite the reverse, in fact: while many teaching texts set out to be funny, the English Teaching Theatre actually succeeds in making students laugh' (Ben Duncan, *ARELS Journal*).

You will naturally be choosing sketches which are generally appropriate to your students' level, and also perhaps because they help to reinforce the practice of particular language areas from the course you are using. You could thus select a sketch according to its structural level, its subject matter, the situation in which it takes place, the functions expressed by the characters or the attitudes the characters adopt, for example. To help you in your selection, this book contains:

- A *Structural levels chart*, which provides a general guide to the structural levels of the sketches.

- An *Index of language areas*, which is an alphabetical list of functions, notions, topics and situations occurring in the sketches.

Using sketches from *English Sketches* 1 and 2

Each sketch has an introductory page of accompanying notes, arranged as follows:

- Brief comments on the background to the sketch.

- **Words and expressions:** some words and expressions occurring in the sketch which you may wish to teach or revise before working with the sketch itself. You may not wish to deal with them *all* beforehand, however, as the students can deduce many meanings in context (and, in some cases, focusing on the words beforehand may spoil the surprise of a joke).

- **Preliminary practice:** ideas for an activity to introduce the sketch. These are usually short oral activities, involving mime, questions and answers, and so on.

- **Follow-up activities:** ideas for activities to use after working with the sketch itself. These are usually further role-playing activities developed from the situation of the sketch.

- **Props and costumes:** notes on props and costumes needed for both a simple classroom re-enacting of the sketch and for a more elaborate performance. For re-enacting in the classroom, these are always simple and easily obtainable objects.

Here are some suggestions as to how you could use the sketches, firstly *in the classroom* (or an English club, for example), where the ultimate aim is not to perform for an outside audience, and secondly *for a performance*.

In the classroom

Having chosen a sketch which you feel is appropriate, you could of course simply play the recording straight through allowing the students to listen, and then move on to the printed script. It is helpful, however, to add other activities to this rather 'bald' approach. Here is a possible sequence.

1 Teach or revise some words and expressions from the sketch as you feel necessary.

2 Do the suggested preliminary practice.

3 Give the students two or three pre-questions, i.e. questions about the sketch for which they will find the answers while listening to the audio-recording. (If it is not possible for you to use the audio-recording, see the *Note* at the end of this section.)

4 Play the audio-recording, perhaps stopping occasionally for predictions (e.g. when a character asks a question, invite the students to guess what the response will be).

5 Follow up on the pre-questions.

6 Play the audio-recording a second time, doing some intensive work on short sections from the sketch (e.g. a few lines of dialogue which include strongly stressed words or special intonation) and/or stopping the recording periodically for students to supply succeeding lines from memory.

7 Distribute photocopies of the script, and move on to the students' re-enacting of the sketch. In small classes, the students can practise the sketch in groups, with each group having the right number of characters for the sketch. They then act out their versions for the rest of the class; if time is short, one group could begin this acting out, then hand over to another group who continue from the point the first group reached, and so on until the sketch has been performed.

In large classes, this re-enacting could be done as follows. Put the students into groups. These groups will contain more students than there are characters in the sketch, but all the students should have something to do, so the groups should be encouraged to add extra characters (even if they only say one line each). The students practise in their groups, and then act out their versions for the rest of the class.

Of course, for these re-enactings in class, it is perfectly all right for the students to have their scripts in their hands – and indeed this is what we would recommend. When the students are familiar with a particular sketch, they may like to try re-enacting it in a freer way, 'in their own words', perhaps based on key words from the different parts of the sketch (written on cue-cards or on the board).

Where necessary, in any re-enacting, male characters can be played by female students, and vice-versa.

8 Finally, you might like to do some of the follow-up activities.

Note: If you are working without the audio-recording, you could start with the printed script of the sketch. Photocopy it and remove some of the words, with Tippex for example; then photocopy this modified version and distribute it to the students, who give their ideas for the missing words. (This idea could also be used when you have the audio-recording: while listening, the students jot down the missing words in the spaces as they hear them. There should only be *short* omissions, and the students can use their own shorthand abbreviations if they like.)

For a performance

Of course, a 'performance' might just be an informal re-enacting, with scripts, in front of other members of the class, or students from other classes. In this case, arrange for the groups to rehearse in private, so that their preparations are not overheard by their 'audience'.

When preparing for a more elaborate performance, such as an end-of-term show, many of the ideas given above for class work will be useful, but there will be other considerations too.

You and the students will need to decide how many sketches are to be performed, who is going to perform them (the less keen 'actors' could have small parts), what else the show might contain – and also what any non-performers are going to do: e.g. they could deliver 'links' in the show (short introductions to the sketches) and help with the preparation of props and costumes. Rehearsals may take place over a fairly lengthy period, when time allows in class or outside class. Of course, the students will actually

have to *learn* the scripts, paying particular attention to clarity, stress and intonation: the audio-recordings will be a useful guide.

The preparation involved in working towards such a performance can be time-consuming, but it and the performance itself can make for an immensely rewarding experience, and contribute greatly to the students' confidence in and enjoyment of English.

And finally…

At the back of this book you will find a few pages headed 'Notes and reminders'. You may like to use these pages in two ways:

- You could use them for your own notes – which sketches worked particularly well with which type of class, useful variations you discovered on the activities suggested, etc.

- When the students are preparing for a performance such as an end-of-term show, you could photocopy them for use as sheets to give to the students, with notes and reminders about rehearsal times, props and costumes which need to be prepared, who is to learn which parts, etc.

Whatever the context in which you use the sketches, we hope that you and your students enjoy working with them, and that the audience, if there is one, enjoys watching them.

Structural levels chart

Although the sketches in Book 1 are designated as *elementary* and those in Book 2 as *intermediate*, all can be used at a variety of levels. As a general guide to the structural levels, the following chart shows the principal verb forms (tenses and related structures) which occur in the sketches.

Book 1

#	Sketch	Present Simple	Present Continuous	Past Simple	Future: going to	Future: will	Present Perfect	Present Perf. Cont.	Past Continuous	Modal aux. +past part
1	Tea break	●								
2	The ticket inspector	●	●	○	○					
3	The King of Boonland	●	●							
4	The restaurant	●	●							
5	The doctor	●	●		○	○	○			
6	Gussett and Rose	●	●	●			○		○	
7	The passport office	●	●	●						
8	Fire practice	●	●	●						
9	The post office	● §	● +	●	○					
10	Mr Jones	●	●	●			○			
11	The shoe stall	● §	●	●		○	○			
12	The check-in desk	●	●	●	○	○	○			
13	The police	● §	●	●			○			
14	Hotel Splendido	● +	● +	●	○	○	○			
15	The bus stop	●	●	●	●	●				
16	A ticket to Birmingham	+ ● §	+ ● §	● O	●	●				

Book 2

#	Sketch	Present Simple	Present Continuous	Past Simple	Future: going to	Future: will	Present Perfect	Present Perf. Cont.	Past Continuous	Modal aux. +past part
1	Gerry Thatcher's party	● +	● +	●	●	●	○			
2	The army	● §	●	●	●	●	○			
3	The dentist	●	●	●	●	●	●			
4	Mr Williams and the postman	●	●	●	●	●	●			○
5	Tourist information	●	●	●	●	●	●			
6	The bank	● §	● §	●	●	●	●			
7	The Superlative vacuum cleaner	●	●	●	●	●	●			
8	Superman and the psychiatrist	●	●	●	●	●	●		○	
9	The lost property office	● §	● §	●	●	●	●			
10	The travel agency	●	●	●	●	●				
11	Gerry Brown's driving test	●	●	●	●	●	●		○	○
12	Giovanni's café	●	●	●	●	●				
13	Shakespeare's house	●	●	●	●	●	●		○	○
14	Mr Universe	●	●	●	●	●	●	○		
15	The new James Bond film	●	●	●	●	●	●	○		
16	World record	●	●	●	●	●	●	●		

● = Occurring freely in sketch. ○ = Occurring in sketch in only one or two instances, which can be treated 'idiomatically'.

+ = Including for 'future arrangements'. § = Including in conditionals or after time conjunctions. O = Including in conditionals.

Index of language areas

This Index lists the main 'language areas' – notions, functions, topics and situations – occurring in the sketches in both Book 1 and Book 2. (The verb forms noted in the Structural levels chart, like other structural points, are only listed here if there are particularly salient occurrences in a given sketch.)

References are given to the book and the sketch. For example, **1** 1 = Book 1, Sketch 1; **2** 8 = Book 2, Sketch 8; etc.

▌Tea break

This sketch was first performed in 1979. Towards the end of the sketch, the stage version included an explanation of the process of making tea, done in the style of a military briefing with a large visual-aid diagram. This has been omitted from the version in this book. We have also amended the end of the sketch for the version here: in the stage version, Tom returned from the café with the orders, but dropped them in the wings at the last minute, and the sketch was then followed by a 1950s-style pastiche song about how to make tea, the 'best drink of the day'.

Words and expressions

café, coffee; kettle, stove, match, gas, teapot; lemon tea, cream cake, whisky and soda

The expression *Come on!* is used when someone has said something unreasonable or hard to believe.

The word *Right* is used several times in the sketch: it is a useful simple way of confirming that you have heard and understood something. Note the other expressions with *right* which occur in the sketch: *All right, Let me get this right, That's right, All right?*

Preliminary practice

In the sketch, one person takes orders for tea, coffee, etc. from a group of people. This is not entirely straightforward as the members of the group change their minds about their orders. You can use this behaviour as a warm-up activity.

Put the students in groups of five. In each group, four students give orders (for tea, coffee, soft drinks and snacks) to the fifth, who tries to remember all the orders without making any notes. Then each of the four makes a small change in their order: for example, they can change white coffee to black coffee, or a cheese sandwich to a ham sandwich. The person taking the orders then tries to remember them again.

Then the process can be repeated, with a different person taking the orders.

Follow-up activities

① Put the students into groups of six. In each group, one person takes orders for drinks and snacks from four others, as in the preliminary practice and in the sketch itself. The sixth person is a café owner.

The four people who give their orders can change their minds as before (more than once if they like!), and the person taking the orders notes them down on a piece of paper. This person then goes to another group and finds the café owner there, improvising with the café owner the conversation about requesting and paying for the drinks and snacks. The café owner can simply supply the drinks and snacks, or can say that certain things are not available and substitute alternatives. The 'order-taker' then returns to his/her original group and delivers the drinks and snacks, with comments about unavailable items as necessary.

② In the sketch, the characters give Tom a series of instructions for making tea (*Put some water in the kettle; Put the kettle on the stove; Light a match,* etc.), with the characters saying one instruction each. The students could give some other sets of instructions in a similar way. These instructions should be for simple tasks, such as making coffee, making a tomato sandwich, or getting to the nearest railway station. The more explicit (or even pedantic) the students make the instructions, the better.

Props and costumes

For simple classroom re-enacting, all that is needed is a table and four chairs. The sketch can be done with or without Tom having a notebook and pencil.

For a more elaborate performance, the table could be brightened up with a tablecloth, and in addition to the four chairs, a tray of strange-looking drinks would be needed for the ending. It is useful if Tom has a notebook and pencil so that he can be seen noting the orders, and crossing out or amending his notes when someone changes their mind or adds something to their order.

Tea break

Scene	A rehearsal room in a theatre
Characters	Five actors taking a tea break: Tom, Jerry, Jane, Martin, Sara

Jerry All right. That's enough. It's time for a cup of tea.

Tom Oh, good. A cup of tea. I can't wait.

Jerry, Jane, Martin and Sara sit down. There is no chair for Tom.

Jane OK, Tom, make the tea.

Tom Me?

Sara Yes, make the tea.

Tom Make the tea? Me?

Jane Why not?

Tom All right. What do I have to do? I mean, how *do* you make tea?

Jerry Huh! He doesn't know how to make tea!

Tom OK, Jerry. How *do* you make tea?

Jerry Er…I don't know.

The others laugh.

Martin Listen, Tom – it's easy. Put some water in the kettle.

Sara Put the kettle on the stove.

Jane Light a match.

Martin Turn on the gas.

Sara And light the gas.

Jane Then put some tea in the teapot –

Tom It sounds a bit complicated.

Jane Oh, come on! It's easy!

Martin Listen, Tom. You don't have to make the tea.

Tom Oh, good.

Martin You can get some from the café.

Tom Oh. OK. See you later.

Tom goes towards the door.

Jerry Wait a minute!

Tom What?

Jane	You don't know what we want yet.
Tom	Oh, yes. Sorry. What do you all want? Sara?
Sara	I'd like a cup of tea – with no milk and no sugar.
Tom	One tea – no milk, no sugar. Jane?
Jane	I'd like a cup of tea – with lots of milk and no sugar.
Tom	Lots of milk – no tea. Right.
Jane	No *sugar*!
Tom	No sugar. Right. Jerry?
Jerry	I'd like a lemon tea and a big cream cake.
Tom	A lemon cake and a cream tea.
Jerry	Careful!
Tom	What do *you* want, Martin?
Martin	A whisky and soda.
Tom	With milk and sugar?
Martin	Of course.

Tom wants to check the orders.

Tom	OK. Let me get this right. Sara, you want a cup of tea, with no milk and no sugar.
Sara	Yes. Oh…No. On second thoughts, I think I'd prefer *coffee*.
Tom	Coffee.
Sara	Yes, a cup of coffee – with milk and sugar.
Tom	Right. So – it's one *coffee* with milk and sugar, and one *tea* with milk and sugar.
Jane	*No* sugar!
Tom	No sugar. Right. Jerry, you want a lemon tea and a big cream cake.
Jerry	That's right.
Tom	And Martin – you want a whisky and soda.
Martin	With milk and sugar.
Tom	With milk and sugar. Right. OK. See you in a minute.

Tom leaves. Very soon, he comes back.

Tom	Right. Here you are. One coffee and soda, one whisky and cream, one lemon and milk, and one big sugar cake. All right?
Jane	Martin?
Martin	Yes?
Jane	Go and make some tea.

The ticket inspector

This sketch was first performed in 1975. It was originally written for the BBC English by Radio series *Let's Speak English*, and then adapted for the ETT's stage show. The script here is exactly as used in the stage show, with one small exception: In the stage show, the names which the passenger uses were varied to suit current affairs (for example, Henry Kissinger, Leonid Brezhnev) and local personalities (for example, the Prime Minister of the country where the performance was taking place, a locally-known pop singer, etc.).

Words and expressions

compartment, passenger, steward, waiter, station, It's in the book (= the rule book), *sir.*

The ambiguity of the expression *first-class* is exploited by the passenger in the sketch: *first-class* is a type of compartment (as opposed to a *second-class* compartment), and can also mean 'excellent'.

Note the use of stress for contrast (e.g. 'I'm not *selling* tickets, sir. I want to *see your* ticket.') and for emphasis (e.g. 'Yes, it *is* very nice, isn't it?').

Preliminary practice

Ask students to write down an occupation on a piece of paper; walk round and make sure that the occupations are different. Collect the pieces of paper and hand them out to different students, and ask them to think about miming the occupation on their piece of paper. Then ask the students to do a double mime to the class: (1) the occupation, and (2) a leisure activity.

From the mimes, the other students should say the occupation, a simple description of what that person does (using the Present Simple tense), and the leisure activity that the person is doing now (using the Present Continuous tense). For example:

Mime 1 (window cleaner) – Class: *You're a window cleaner. You clean windows.*
Mime 2 (watching TV) – Class: *You're watching TV.*

Follow-up activities

① In the sketch, the passenger refuses coffee and dinner. The students could improvise dialogues in which the passenger does not refuse, but buys something from the steward and makes some enquiries of the waiter; like this, for example:

With the steward: Buy a coffee. Ask what sandwiches there are. Choose one. Pay. Ask what time the train arrives at its destination.

With the waiter: Ask what time dinner is served until. Ask how much it costs. Ask what is on the menu. Ask if the train is on time.

② The students could improvise some dialogues in situations which are parallel to the sketch, such as:

Policeman, car-driver: Driver has no licence. Customs officer, traveller: Traveller has no passport. Stadium attendant, football supporter: Football supporter has no ticket.

The dialogues can follow a similar development to the sketch, incorporating the students' own ideas.

③ The students could improvise either of these conversations, after the passenger has left the train:

The man meets a friend at the station, and describes the events on the train.
The ticket inspector has a cup of tea in the buffet, and tells the steward and waiter about the events.

Props and costumes

Whether for simple classroom re-enacting or for a more elaborate performance, two chairs facing one another will represent the compartment very well. The passenger should have a newspaper (or magazine or book) and the inspector a pencil and small notebook, kept in a pocket until needed. The students should be encouraged to mime opening and closing the door, glancing out of the window, and so on.

For a performance, a peaked hat and uniform jacket are needed for the inspector, as well as costumes for the waiter and the steward; the steward may also have a tray with coffee on it.

The ticket inspector

Scene   A compartment on a train
Characters   A passenger on a train
    A ticket inspector
    A steward and a waiter

The passenger is sitting in a compartment on a train. He is reading a newspaper. The steward opens the door.

Steward   Coffee!

Passenger   No, thanks.

The passenger closes the door, and continues reading. The waiter opens the door.

Waiter   Seats for dinner!

Passenger   No, thanks.

The passenger closes the door again, and continues reading. The ticket inspector opens the door.

Inspector   Tickets!

Passenger   No, thanks.

Inspector   Pardon?

Passenger   I don't want a ticket, thank you.

Inspector   I'm not *selling* tickets, sir.

Passenger   No?

Inspector   No, I want to *see your* ticket.

Passenger   Oh, I haven't got a ticket.

Inspector   You haven't got a ticket?

Passenger   No. I never buy a ticket.

Inspector   Why not?

Passenger   Well, they *are* very expensive, you know.

Inspector   Sir, you're travelling on a train. When people travel on a train, they always buy a ticket.

Passenger   Er –

Inspector   And *this* is a first-class compartment.

Passenger   Yes, it *is* very nice, isn't it?

Inspector   No, sir. I mean: This is a *first-class* compartment. When people travel in a first-class compartment, they always buy a first-class ticket.

© Doug Case, Ken Wilson 1995. Published by Heinemann English Language Teaching. This sheet may be photocopied and used within the class.

They look at each other for a moment.

Passenger   No, they don't.

Inspector   What?

Passenger   A lot of people don't buy tickets. The Queen doesn't buy a ticket, does she? Eh? Eh?

Inspector   No, sir, but *she's* a famous person.

Passenger   And what about you? Where's yours?

Inspector   Mine?

Passenger   Yes, yours. Your ticket. Have *you* got a ticket?

Inspector   Me, sir?

Passenger   Yes, you.

Inspector   No, I haven't got a ticket.

Passenger   Ooh – are you a famous person?

Inspector   (**Flattered**) Famous? Well, not very – (**Back to normal**) Sir, *I* am a ticket inspector. I inspect tickets. Are you going to show me your ticket?

Passenger   No, I haven't got a ticket.

Inspector   I see.

The ticket inspector puts his hand into his pocket.

Passenger   What are you going to do?

Inspector   I'm going to write your name in my book.

Passenger   Oh.

Inspector   What is your name, sir?

Passenger   Mickey Mouse.

The inspector begins to write.

Inspector   Mickey –

Passenger   – Mouse. M-O-U-S-E.

The inspector stops writing.

Inspector   Your *name*, sir?

Passenger   Karl Marx? William Shakespeare? Charles Dickens?

Inspector   I see, sir. Well, if you're not going to tell me your name, please leave the train.

Passenger   Pardon?

Inspector   Leave the train.

Passenger   I can't.

Inspector   You can't what?

Passenger   I can't leave the train.

Inspector   Why not?

Passenger	It's moving.
Inspector	Not *now*, sir. At the next station.
Passenger	Oh.
Inspector	It's in the book, sir. When you travel by train, you buy a ticket, and if you don't buy a ticket, you –
Passenger / **Inspector**	} – leave the train.
Inspector	Here we are, sir. We're coming to a station. Please leave the train now.
Passenger	Now?
Inspector	Yes, sir. I'm sorry, but –
Passenger	Oh, that's OK.
Inspector	– it's in the book, and – What did you say?
Passenger	I said: 'That's OK.'
Inspector	OK?
Passenger	Yes, this is my station. Goodbye.

The passenger leaves the train.

Having decided to write a sketch including the language used for describing or finding out about a country, we invented a mythical country in the middle of the Atlantic Ocean, whose king visits Buckingham Palace. The sketch was first performed in 1981, coinciding with the marriage of Prince Charles and Lady Diana Spencer. In the stage version, the King of Boonland had come to Buckingham Palace to bring the happy couple greetings from Boonland. This has been modified for the version in this book.

Words and expressions

prove, coin, note, change, good wishes, present (= gift), map, ocean, population, capital

The words *boono, boonito* and *Boonese* are of course invented, and the students will deduce their meaning from the context and by reference to *Boonland*.

Several Object clauses occur in the sketch (e.g. 'I think *he's deaf*'; 'I can prove *I'm the King of Boonland*'; 'You don't know *where Boonland is?*'); these should not pose any comprehension problems.

Preliminary practice

Draw the outline of a real or imaginary country on the board. If it is a real country, ask the class if they can recognize the outline. Then ask the class what they would like to know about the country. Write their answers on the board: *capital city, population, currency*, etc. Then elicit what questions would be asked to find out this information. Encourage the class to find more than one way of asking the same thing, e.g. *What's the population?* or *How many people live there?*

If the country is real, but was not guessed from its outline, you can then reveal its name. If the country was imaginary, tell the class that they are now going to find out such things about the imaginary country of Boonland.

Follow-up activities

① Once familiar with the sketch, the students could work in groups to invent and enact their own sketch with a parallel structure. For example:

A visitor from another imaginary country tries to get into 10 Downing Street, past the policeman at the door, in order to see the British Prime Minister.

Or: The sketch could be set in the students' country, with the visitor being an eccentric British tourist.

② The students could do some research in dictionaries, encyclopedias or reference books about countries where English is a first or official language (e.g. Australia, New Zealand, the USA, Canada, India, Nigeria). Individual students or pairs/groups of students should take one country each. They might like to complete a form, like this, for example:

Name of country: ....
Location: ....
Head of state: ....
Population: ....
Capital city: ....
Language(s): ....
Unit of currency: ....

The students could also add any other interesting items of information they discover. When they have gathered the information, they can give a brief talk to the class.

Props and costumes

For classroom re-enacting, these props are useful: a book (to represent the map), pieces of paper (the *boono* notes), a coin (the *boonito*), a rolled sheet of paper (the banana); the King can carry his things in a plastic bag, and produce them when relevant. The guard may like to use a broom as a rifle.

For a more elaborate performance, improved versions of the props above will be needed, including a real or plastic banana. In our stage version, the coin was very large. Costumes: a uniform for the guard, possibly including a red tunic and the tall furry helmet called a 'busby'; our King had a crown, but apart from that was rather absurdly dressed (garish shirt, baggy shorts, football socks and tennis shoes).

The King of Boonland

Scene	In front of Buckingham Palace
Characters	A guard
	A sergeant
	The King of Boonland

The guard and the sergeant march to the sentry-box.

Sergeant	Quick march! Left, right, left, right, left, right, left, right! Halt!…Right turn!…Bradshaw!
Guard	Sir!
Sergeant	You are guarding Buckingham Palace.
Guard	Yes, sir!
Sergeant	Don't forget!
Guard	No, sir!

The sergeant leaves. The guard stands silently. The King of Boonland comes up to the guard.

King	Good morning…Hello?…Nice day, isn't it?…Do you speak English?…Sprechen Sie español?…I think he's deaf. Oh, well…

The King starts to go into the Palace.

Guard	Oi!
King	Oh! He can talk!
Guard	Where are you going?
King	I'm going into Buckingham Palace.
Guard	Stand there!
King	I don't want to stand there. I want to go in there.
Guard	Stand there!!
King	Oh, all right.
Guard	Who do you think you are?
King	I'm Fred, King of Boonland.
Guard	Well, listen to me, Fred King –
King	No, no, my name isn't Fred King. I am King Fred.
Guard	Are you trying to tell me that *you* are a real king?
King	Yes. I am the King of Boonland.
Guard	Boonland?
King	Yes.

Guard	And where exactly is Boonland?
King	Huh! You don't know where Boonland is?
Guard	No.
King	Oh. OK, look at my map…

The King finds his map.

King	…yes, here we are. Now, this is a map of the world.
Guard	Yes.
King	And Boonland is *here*.
Guard	*That* is the Atlantic Ocean.
King	Yes – and Boonland is in the middle.
Guard	What? In the middle of the Atlantic?
King	Yes.
Guard	I don't believe you.
King	Eh?
Guard	I think you are trying to get into Buckingham Palace.
King	That's right. I am.
Guard	Well, you can't.
King	Yes, I can. Wait a minute – I can prove I'm the King of Boonland. Look!
Guard	It's a five-pound note.
King	No, it's not five *pounds*.
Guard	Isn't it?
King	No, it's five *boonos*.
Guard	Five *boonos*?
King	Yes.

The guard looks at the note.

Guard	Oh, yes! Five boonos. So this is the money you use in Boonland.
King	Yes, it is.
Guard	How many boonos are there in a pound?
King	Half a million.
Guard	Half a million?
King	Yes, and there are one hundred *boonitos* in a boono.
Guard	Now, listen to me –
King	Ah! I can prove I'm the King of Boonland. There's a picture of me on the one-boonito coin. Um…Have you got change for ten boonitos?
Guard	No, I haven't!
King	Oh. It's all right. Look – one boonito coin, with a picture of me on it.

Guard	Oh, yes. A picture of you.

The King nods.

Guard	Tell me – why do you want to go into the Palace?
King	I am here to bring the Queen the good wishes of the people of Boonland.
Guard	The good wishes of the people of Boonland?
King	Yes.
Guard	How many people are there in Boonland?
King	Well, there's *me*, and *my mother*, and –
Guard	No, No! *All together*! What's the *population* of Boonland?
King	Ah – well, there are the people in the capital –
Guard	In the capital?
King	Yes, Boonland City. And there are the people who live in the mountains – we call them 'the mountain people'.
Guard	Very clever.
King	And there are the people who live in the lake.
Guard	In the lake?!
King	Yes.
Guard	What do you call them?
King	Stupid.

They laugh.

Guard	So, there are the people in the capital –
King	Boonland City.
Guard	– and the people who live in the mountains –
King	The mountain people.
Guard	– and the people who live in the lake.
King	The idiots.
Guard	How many is that all together?
King	Um…Fourteen.
Guard	Fourteen?!
King	Yes. And we want to give the Queen a special Boonese present.
Guard	A special present from Boonland?
King	Yes – here it is!

The King takes a banana from his bag.

Guard	But that's a banana.
King	I know.
Guard	What's so special about a banana?

King	It isn't an ordinary banana.
Guard	Isn't it?
King	No. Put it in your ear.
Guard	What?!
King	Put the banana in your ear.
Guard	Why?
King	Just put the banana in your ear!
Guard	All right.

The guard puts the banana in his ear.

King	Can you hear anything?
Guard	Oh, yes!
King	What does it sound like?
Guard	It sounds like an elephant with toothache.
King	What?! *That* is the National Song of Boonland. (**He sings**) Oh, Boonland! */!*&*@::!*/!*
Guard	Oi!
King	It's all right – I'm speaking Boonese. */!* is a word in Boonese.
Guard	And what exactly does */!* mean?
King	It means 'land of sunshine and bananas'.

The King sneezes.

Guard	What does *that* mean?
King	It means I've got a bad cold. Now give me the banana, because I don't want to be late for tea with the Queen.
Guard	Oh, right, sir. Here you are, sir.

The guard gives back the banana.

King	Thank you very much. Oh, this is for you.
Guard	What is it?
King	Half a million boonos.
Guard	Half a million boonos?!
King	Yes. Go and buy yourself a cup of tea.

4 The restaurant

This sketch was first performed in 1979, and since then there have been several stage versions, including one in which a customer had lost her voice and the restaurant had no written menu, thus necessitating the use of a lot of mime to order the meal. Also, in most versions, music was actually supplied by Manfred Schmidt, the Spanish guitarist, in the form of a song which followed the sketch itself. The version in this book is a combination of elements from the various stage versions.

Words and expressions

trattoria, reservation, food, menu, manager, service (not) included, take-away service, Look here (used to begin an objection)

Note the expressions *It must be a mistake* (used to refer to a specific mistake – here, a misprint) and *There must be some mistake* (used when trying to resolve a confusion or a misunderstanding in a conversation). Also note the formal tone of *Allow me to…* and the ironic tone of *I don't know. I only work here.*

Preliminary practice

Here is an activity using mime to show what you want to eat, as if in a restaurant, having lost your voice.

Put the class into pairs or groups and then give each group a piece of paper on which is written a three-course menu. (The menus for the various pairs or groups should be different, although some dishes may appear on more than one menu.) Give the students a few moments to think about how they could mime the dishes so that someone else would understand.

The groups then mime their dishes for the rest of the class to guess. Group mime takes away the threat of embarrassment, and allows students to help each other by adding extra information.

Follow-up activities

① In groups (of four, for example), the students could simply practise ordering from a menu. One student is the waiter and the others the customers, ordering and asking for explanations as necessary. You could provide simple menus, like this:

MENU
Starters
| Tomato soup | Prawn cocktail | Grapefruit juice |
Main dishes
| Roast beef | Grilled chicken | Fish pie |
Desserts
| Ice-cream | Apple pie | Fresh fruit |

The students could add their own ideas to the menus, e.g. invented dishes such as 'vampireburgers' which will definitely need some explanation from the waiter.

② The students could build on the preliminary practice activity and produce a sketch like our earlier version mentioned in the introductory note above: The students work in pairs; in each pair, one student is the waiter in a restaurant which has no written menu; the other student is a customer who has lost his/her voice. The customers thus have to explain what they want, ask questions, etc. entirely in mime, and the waiters have to work out what is intended. The sketch should comprise arriving, asking for a table for one, finding that there is no written menu, miming the dishes desired (a starter, a main dish, a dessert, and a drink), eating, paying the bill and leaving.

Props and costumes

For classroom re-enacting, these props are useful: a newspaper (or a sheet of paper to represent it), perhaps with the details which **B** reads out to **A** pasted inside it; a table and two chairs; a piece of paper or card (the menu); a pencil; and a sandwich in cellophane (or something to represent it, e.g. a book). Manfred can mime his guitar.

For a more elaborate performance, improved versions of the props listed above will be needed, e.g. an English newspaper if possible; a tablecloth and items on the table (cutlery, possibly a vase of flowers, etc.), a guitar. Costumes: normal clothes for the customers; perhaps a smart dinner-jacket for the manager; a cabaret costume for Manfred, perhaps with some Spanish and some German elements.

The restaurant

Scene	The customers' home in London, and then a restaurant in London
Characters	Customer A
	Customer B
	The manager of the restaurant
	Manfred Schmidt, a Spanish guitarist

A and B are at home.

Customer A   Let's go to a restaurant tonight.

Customer B   OK.

Customer A   Somewhere different.

Customer B   All right. Let's have a look in the newspaper.

B opens the newspaper.

Customer B   Er… Cinemas…Theatres…Restaurants. Ooh, this sounds nice. (**Reading**) 'London's newest restaurant. The *Trattoria Romantica*.'

Customer A   It sounds good.

Customer B   'The *Trattoria Romantica*. The best French restaurant in London.'

Customer A   French?

Customer B   Yes.

Customer A   '*Trattoria Romantica*' sounds Italian.

Customer B   It says *French* here.

Customer A   What else does it say?

Customer B   'Open every evening –'

Customer A   Good.

Customer B   '– from 7.30 to 7.45.'

Customer A   What? Fifteen minutes?

Customer B   It must be a mistake.

Customer A   I hope so. Anything else?

Customer B   Yes. 'Music every evening –'

Customer A   Good.

Customer B   '– from our Spanish guitarist –'

Customer A   Spanish guitarist?

Customer B   '– Manfred Schmidt.'

Customer A   Manfred Schmidt?!

Customer B   Yes. Oh, and there's a picture of the manager.

Customer A	What's his name?
Customer B	Stavros Papadopoulos.
Customer A	Stavros Papadopoulos?
Customer B	Yes.
Customer A	But that's a *Greek* name.
Customer B	Yes.
Customer A	So it's an *Italian* restaurant, serving *French* food…The *Spanish* guitarist has got a *German* name…And the manager's *Greek*.
Customer B	That's right. It sounds very international. Let's try it.
Customer A	All right.

Later. They arrive at the restaurant.

Customer B	Well, here we are – the *Trattoria Romantica*.
Customer A	There's no one here. (**Calling**) Hello?

The manager appears. He is not very friendly.

Manager	Yes?
Customer A	Oh, good evening. Is this the *Trattoria Romantica*?
Manager	I don't know. I only work here.
Customer A	Pardon?
Manager	Yes, yes, yes. This is the *Trattoria Romantica*, but we're closed for lunch.
Customer B	Closed for lunch? But it's nine o'clock.
Manager	Ah. In that case, we're closed for breakfast.
Customer B	It's nine o'clock in the *evening*.
Manager	(**Friendly**) Yes, of course it is. Just a little joke. Allow me to introduce myself. I am Stavros Papadopoulos, the manager of the *Trattoria Romantica*. What can I do for you?
Customer B	We'd like a table for two, please.
Manager	Have you got a reservation?
Customer B	Er…No.
Manager	Ah. That's a problem.
Customer A	But the restaurant is empty.
Manager	Is it? Oh, yes. Er…a table for two…

He looks around the restaurant.

Manager	Yes. Here you are – a lovely table for two.
Customer A	Thank you.

A and B sit down at the table.

Manager	Is everything all right?

Customer B	Yes, thank you.
Manager	Good. That's £12.50, please.
Customer B	What?
Manager	£12.50.
Customer A	What for?
Manager	For the chairs.
Customer A	The chairs?!
Manager	Yes – £6.25 each.
Customer B	There must be some mistake.
Manager	Oh, sorry – £6.30. That's £12.60 altogether. And of course £37 for the table.
Customer B	£37 for the table?!
Manager	That's...er...£49.60 altogether.
Customer A	Look here –
Manager	Service not included.
Customer B	Service?!
Manager	Would you like to pay separately or together?
Customer A	Look – we don't *want* the table or the chairs.
Manager	Oh, you want to sit on the floor.
Customer B	No, we don't want to *take* them *away*.
Manager	That's good. We don't have a take-away service.
Customer B	We want to sit here and eat something.
Manager	Eat something?
Customer B	Yes.
Manager	Ah.
Customer B	Can we see the menu, please?
Manager	Er...yes. There you are.

He gives them a very small menu.

Customer A	It's a very small menu.
Manager	It's a very small restaurant. Now, what would you like?
Customer B	(**Looking at the menu**) Let's see...(**Reading**) 'Egg and chips. Double egg and chips. Double egg and double chips.'
Customer A	Um...Isn't this a *French* restaurant?
Manager	Oh, yes. Sorry. Give me the menu.

The manager takes the menu.

Manager	Thank you. Have you got a pencil?
Customer B	Here you are.

B gives the manager a pencil.

Manager   Thank you.

He writes on the menu.

Manager   There – a French menu.

He gives the menu back to B.

Customer B   (**Reading**) 'Oeuf et pommes frites. Deux oeufs et pommes frites. Deux oeufs et deux pommes frites.'

B puts the menu on the table.

Customer A   What if you don't like eggs?

Manager   Have the chips.

Customer B   What if you don't like chips?

Manager   Have the eggs.

Customer A   What if you don't like eggs or chips?

Manager   Have a sandwich.

Customer B   A sandwich?

Manager   Yes. I've got one here in my pocket.

He puts a sandwich on the table.

Customer B   Thank you. Er…what's *in* this sandwich?

Manager   Sand.

Customer A
Customer B } Sand?!

Manager   Yes, sand. That's why it's called a sandwich – because of the sand which is inside it.

Customer A   (**To B**) Come on, let's go.

Manager   What's the matter? You're not going already, are you?

Customer B   Yes.

Manager   Why?

Customer A   Because this must be the worst restaurant in London.

Manager   No, it isn't.

Customer B   Isn't it?

Manager   No. I've got another one round the corner. It's much worse than this one. Anyway, people don't come here for the food.

Customer A   I'm not surprised.

Manager   No, they come here for the music.

Customer B   The music?

Manager   Yes. Allow me to present Manfred Schmidt and his Spanish guitar.

© Doug Case, Ken Wilson 1995. Published by Heinemann English Language Teaching. This sheet may be photocopied and used within the class.

Manfred comes in with his guitar.

Manfred   Olé! Guten Abend, meine Damen und Herren!

Customer A   Stavros?

Manager   Yes?

Customer A   What can Manfred play?

Manager   Anything you like.

Customer A   Really?

Manager   Yes, anything at all.

Customer A   Good. Tell him to play football.

Manager   Football? What do you mean?

Customer A   We're leaving. Goodbye.

Manager   Oh, goodbye. Do come again. Don't forget to tell your friends!

A and B leave the restaurant.

Manager   That's the trouble with English people, Manfred.

Manfred   What's that, Stavros?

Manager   They don't know a good restaurant when they see one.

© Doug Case, Ken Wilson 1995. Published by Heinemann English Language Teaching. This sheet may be photocopied and used within the class.

5 The doctor

Over the years, we have written several sketches set in doctors' consulting-rooms. The first was in 1978 and involved two patients who always spoke together, saying exactly the same thing; in 1986, we had a sketch concerning two rather disconcerting surgeons. The sketch in this book was first performed in 1988. We have simplified the opening section somewhat: the stage version involves considerable confusion between the telephone, a banana in a fruit-bowl, knocking at the door and the student having entered the room while the doctor thinks she is still on the phone.

Words and expressions

student-doctor, patient, examine, take (someone's) temperature, feel (someone's) pulse, arm, back, cough (vb./n.), remedy (n.), rub

The sketch includes a pun on the word patient, as a noun, meaning someone visiting a doctor, and as an adjective, meaning the opposite of 'impatient'. The word wrong occurs in several expressions: Find out what's wrong, There's nothing wrong with…, I know what's wrong with him.

Preliminary practice

Collections of jokes often include a lot about doctors. Find some which consist of just two lines – the patient speaking and the doctor replying – like these:

Doctor, I've swallowed a pencil: what shall I do? – Use a pen.
Doctor, I think I've become invisible. – Who said that?
Doctor, no one is interested in me. – Next!
Doctor, I've had this problem before. – Well, you've got it again.

Write the doctor's utterances on individual pieces of paper, and do the same for the patient's utterances. Distribute the pieces of paper to the students, who then find the person with the other half of their joke. When the pairs have been formed, they can deliver their jokes so the whole class can hear them.

Follow-up activities

① In pairs, the students could improvise some conversations between a patient and a doctor. Before starting, the patients decide what is wrong with them, and how long they have had the problem – or this information could be provided on cue-cards. In the conversations, the doctors should ask questions to find out about the problems, the patients should ask for advice about treatment, and the doctors should give some advice. (The advice need not always be serious; it could be to take a holiday, to find a new job, or to move to a different house, for example, even if this is inappropriate to the patients' problems.) Finally, the patients thank the doctors and leave.

② The previous activity could be expanded into an activity for groups of three students: one student is a patient, another is the doctor's receptionist, and the third is the doctor. In each group, the patient 'telephones' the receptionist and makes an appointment to see the doctor. The patient then arrives and tells the receptionist about the appointment. The receptionist takes the patient in to see the doctor, and the activity proceeds as before.

③ A variation (using either of the formats above) would be to set the sketch at a vet's, with the customers bringing a sick animal rather than being patients at a doctor's.

Props and costumes

For simple classroom re-enacting, all that is needed is a table, two chairs, and a sheet of paper (the list of questions); a telephone on the table is useful, and the patient may like to improvise a sling (using a scarf, for example).

For a performance, improved versions of those props will be needed (the list of questions could be on a clipboard, the patient should have a proper sling, and note that the telephone has to ring), plus a stethoscope and bottle of medicine for the doctor. Costumes: white coats for the doctor and student-doctor; clothes for the patient as desired.

The doctor

Scene A doctor's consulting-room
Characters The doctor
A student-doctor
A patient

The doctor is sitting at his desk. The telephone rings: the student-doctor is calling.

Doctor Hello?

Student Doctor Watson?

Doctor Yes?

Student My name's Smith.

Doctor What's the matter with you?

Student Nothing, doctor. I'm fine.

Doctor Really? In that case, why are you calling?

Student Well, I'm a doctor.

Doctor You're a doctor?

Student Actually, I'm a student-doctor.

Doctor You're a student?

Student – doctor.

Doctor Yes?

Student Er…I'm a student-doctor.

Doctor Ah! A student-doctor!

Student Yes, I'm studying to be a doctor, doctor.

Doctor A doctor-doctor? What's a doctor-doctor?

Student Well, *you're* a doctor, doctor.

Doctor Am I?

Student Yes, and I'd like to come and watch you working.

Doctor Fine. Come any time. Goodbye.

The doctor puts the telephone down. There is a knock at the door.

Doctor Come in!

The patient enters. He has one arm in a sling.

Patient Good morning, doctor.

Doctor (**To the patient**) Ah, you must be the student-doctor.

Patient   Pardon?

Doctor   Student-doctor.

Patient   Student-doctor? No, actually, I'm –

Doctor   Sit down.

The patient sits down.

Doctor   Now, you want to watch me working.

Patient   Er…No, actually, I'm not a –

There is another knock at the door.

Doctor   Ah. That'll be my first patient. Come in!

The student-doctor comes in.

Student   Good morning, doctor.

Doctor   Good morning. (**To the student-doctor, indicating the patient**) This is a student-doctor. He's come to watch me working. (**To the patient, indicating the student-doctor**) This is a patient. I'm going to ask her a few questions.

Student   Doctor?

Doctor   Yes?

Student   *I'm* a student-doctor.

Doctor   Really?

Student   Yes.

Doctor   (**To the patient, indicating the student-doctor**) She's a student-doctor. Like you.

Patient   I'm not a student-doctor.

Doctor   You're not a student?

Patient   – doctor.

Doctor   Yes?

Student   I think he's a patient, doctor.

Doctor   A patient doctor? That's marvellous! Patient doctors are the best kind.

Student   No! *I'm* a student-doctor – *he's* a patient.

Doctor   I'm a student-doctor – he's a patient.

Patient   No! *I'm* a patient – *you're* a doctor.

Doctor   I'm a patient – you're a doctor.

Patient
Student   } No!!

Student   *You're* a doctor – *he's* a patient!

Doctor   You're a doctor – he's a patient!

Patient
Student   } No!!

Patient   *You're* a doctor – *she's* a student-doctor.

© Doug Case, Ken Wilson 1995. Published by Heinemann English Language Teaching. This sheet may be photocopied and used within the class.

Doctor	You're a doctor – she's a student-doctor.
Patient **Student**	} No!!
Student	(***Indicating***) Student-doctor…doctor…patient, doctor.
Patient	(***Indicating***) Patient…doctor…student-doctor, doctor.
Doctor	(***Pointing in various directions***) Doctor, doctor, doctor, doctor, doctor, doctor! (***Indicating correctly***) Patient…doctor…student-doctor.
Patient **Student**	} Yes!!
Doctor	Well, I'm glad that's all clear. Goodbye.
Student	Doctor?
Doctor	Yes?
Student	I think you should examine the patient.
Doctor	Examine him?
Student	Find out what's wrong.
Doctor	What a good idea! Now, when you examine a patient, the first thing you must do is tell the patient to sit down. You try it.
Student	(***To the patient***) Sit down.
Patient	I'm already sitting down.
Student	He's already sitting down.
Doctor	Ah, this is a very common problem. If the patient is already sitting down, *don't* tell him to sit down.
Student	Oh. (***To the patient***) Don't sit down.
Patient	Oh. Right.

The patient stands up.

Doctor	Sit down!
Patient	Right.

The patient sits down.

Doctor	Now, when the patient is sitting down, what's the first thing you should do?
Student	Take his temperature?

She feels the patient's forehead.

Doctor	No.
Student	Feel his pulse?

She feels the patient's pulse (on his good arm).

Doctor	No.
Student	Tell him to say 'Aah'?

Doctor	Pardon?
Student	Say 'Aah'.
Doctor	'Aah!'
Student	No – him.
Doctor	'Himmm!'
Student	No! Tell *him* to say '*Aah*'.
Doctor	Ah! Him! (**To the patient**) Say 'Aah'.
Patient	Pardon?
Doctor	Say 'Aah'.
Patient	Aah.
Doctor	Good!
Patient	Actually, doctor, the problem is my arm –
Doctor	Now we can ask the patient some questions.
Student	Questions?
Doctor	Yes – and here they are.

The doctor gives the student-doctor a list of questions.

Doctor	Go on – you can ask him the questions.
Student	Oh. Right.
Doctor	(**To the patient**) Now listen very carefully, because we have some very important questions for you.
Patient	But doctor, the problem is –
Doctor	(**To the student-doctor**) Read the first question.
Student	Are you Mrs Elisabeth Robinson of 45 Shakespeare Avenue?
Patient	No.
Doctor	Correct.
Student	Is this your first baby?
Patient	What?
Doctor	Try the next one.
Student	What is the capital of Uruguay?
Patient	Montevideo.
Doctor	Correct. Well, there's nothing wrong with his South American geography.
Patient	But doctor –
Doctor	You're fine. You can go now.
Student	Doctor!
Doctor	Yes?
Student	I really think you should examine the patient.
Doctor	Good idea.

The doctor places his stethoscope on the patient's chest.

Doctor   Cough.

The patient coughs.

Doctor   Cough.

The patient coughs.

Doctor   Cough.

The patient coughs.

Doctor   Cough.

The patient coughs.

Doctor   Cough.

The patient coughs.

Doctor   I know what's wrong with him.

Student   What?

Doctor   He's got a cough.

Student   He's got a cough?!

Doctor   Yes – and I, Doctor Watson, have got the answer.

The doctor produces a bottle of medicine from his pocket.

Doctor   (*Pointing at the bottle*) 'Doctor Watson's Universal Cough Remedy.'

Student   'Doctor Watson's Universal *Cough* Remedy'?

Doctor   Yes.

Student   But what about his *arm*?

Doctor   Er… (*Pointing at the bottle again*) 'Doctor Watson's Universal Cough *and Arm* Remedy.'

Student   'Universal Cough *and Arm* Remedy'?

Doctor   Yes – and this is how it works. He can drink it –

He makes the patient drink some of the medicine.

Patient   Aaargh!

Doctor   – but it tastes horrible. *Or* he can rub it on his back –

He rubs some of the medicine on the patient's back.

Doctor   – but he must mix it with water first.

Patient   Aa…aaa…aaargh!

Doctor As you can see, he's feeling much better now. All he needs is six months in hospital. Let's take him away.

Student Where? To the hospital?

Doctor No, to the bus stop. Come on!

The doctor and the student-doctor help the patient to his feet, and they all leave.

© Doug Case, Ken Wilson 1995. Published by Heinemann English Language Teaching. This sheet may be photocopied and used within the class.

Gussett and Rose

6

This sketch was first performed in 1975. It began as a dialogue written for the Belgian magazine for learners of English, *English Pages*. The idea was to have a dialogue which *ended* with the words 'How do you do?', rather than *beginning* with those words. This dialogue was then rewritten for the ETT's stage show, and used as a short link between two sketches. It proved a popular item with audiences and was expanded slightly to become a sketch in its own right.

Words and expressions

wife, married; Army, Navy, architect, taxi-driver, How are you, then? (= So, how are you?), *Actually,…/…, as a matter of fact.* (used when correcting someone)

The sketch includes a number of idiomatic expressions: *Goodness me!* and *Well I never!*, expressing surprise; *It's a small world*, commenting on a coincidence; *Doesn't time fly!* and *It seems like yesterday…*, commenting on the passage of time.

Preliminary practice

The two characters in the sketch ask each other a lot of questions in an attempt to find out if they have met before. So a simple game of 'Twenty Questions' will be useful preparation for the students.

Ask individual students to think of a famous person (preferably someone who is still alive). The rest of the class then ask the individual students questions to find out who their famous person is. Questions must be the kind which can be answered *Yes* or *No*, rather than questions beginning *What…?, Where…?*, etc.

Remember that it is always better for the students to 'be' their famous person, so that the questions are of the type *Are you a politician?, Do you live in this country?*, and so on (rather than *Is he/she a politician?, Does he/she live in this country?*, and so on).

Follow-up activities

① For some further practice of meeting and introducing people, put the students into groups of three: student **A** will be the 'introducer'; students **B** and **C** have not met before. Give each group a set of cue-cards which assign particular identities to **B** and **C**: their names, the cities in which they live, their jobs and their hobbies. **A** is given details which are not all correct, so that **B** and **C** will have to correct the introductions. Here are examples of what the cue-cards could look like:

CARD FOR B	CARD FOR A		CARD FOR C
Albert Smith.	Arthur Smith.	Doris Brown.	Dora Brown.
Born in Liverpool,	Liverpool.	Birmingham.	Birmingham.
living in London.	Teacher.	Nurse.	Doctor.
Retired teacher.	Climbing.	Swimming.	Skiing.
Climbing.	⬅	➡	

② Put the students into pairs. Each student imagines that they have to introduce their partner as a celebrity on a TV show, and writes a few lines as their 'script' for doing this. (Real names can be kept, but other details – job, nationality, etc. – must be invented.) The students do not show their 'script' to their partners or to other members of the class. Then each student introduces their celebrity to the rest of the class; the celebrities deny each piece of information given about them; for example:

- I'd like to introduce Sergio Rossi, the film actor.
- Actually, I'm not a film actor – I'm a film **director**.

Props and costumes

This sketch needs no props at all, either for simple classroom re-enacting or for a more elaborate performance.

For a performance, costumes can be as desired by the students. The only limitations are that the two characters are English, and that, when they meet, they are outdoors (in the street) – thus they could be wearing outdoor clothes, perhaps including hats, for example.

Gussett and Rose

Scene   A street
Characters   Two Englishmen: Albert Gussett and Harold Rose

The two men pass in the street.

Rose   Goodness me!

Gussett   Well I never!

Rose   Herbert Bishop!

Gussett   Arthur Trigwell!

Rose   No…Actually my name's Harold Rose.

Gussett   I'm Albert Gussett, as a matter of fact.

Rose   Albert Gussett. Of course.

Gussett   And you're Harold Rose. Of course you are.

Rose   Well I never!

Gussett   Goodness me!

They hesitate for a moment.

Rose   Well, how are you, then?

Gussett   Fine, fine. How's Alice?

Rose   Alice?

Gussett   Yes, Alice. Your wife's name's Alice, isn't it?

Rose   No, no…Gloria, actually.

Gussett   Oh, yes. Gloria Trigwell.

Rose   Er…Rose.

Gussett   Rose Trigwell?

Rose   No. Gloria Rose.

Gussett   Gloria Rose. Of course. How is she?

Rose   She's very well. How's…er…

Gussett   Doris?

Rose   Yes, Doris, your wife. How is she?

Gussett   Oh, she's very well –

Rose   Good, good.

Gussett   – but she isn't my wife.

Rose   No?

© Doug Case, Ken Wilson 1995. Published by Heinemann English Language Teaching. This sheet may be photocopied and used within the class.

Gussett	I'm not married.
Rose	Oh.
Gussett	Doris is my sister.
Rose	Oh, yes.

They hesitate again for a moment.

Rose	Well, it *is* a small world, isn't it, Herbert?
Gussett	Albert.
Rose	Albert, yes. It seems like yesterday –
Gussett	Yes, it certainly does…
Rose	– when we were at that awful school together.
Gussett	School?
Rose	Yes. Doesn't time fly?
Gussett	We weren't at school together.
Rose	Do you remember that awful English teacher with black teeth?
Gussett	We *weren't* at school together.
Rose	Weren't we?
Gussett	No, we were in the Army together.
Rose	We weren't.
Gussett	Weren't we?
Rose	I was in the Navy.
Gussett	Oh.

They hesitate again for a moment.

Rose	Er…Albert, I mean *Herbert* –
Gussett	No, no, Albert's my name.
Rose	Er, yes…Albert, how *do* we know each other?
Gussett	I was just wondering about that myself, er…
Rose	Harold.
Gussett	Yes, Harold. Er…Are you an architect?
Rose	Yes! Are *you* an architect?
Gussett	No, I'm a taxi-driver.
Rose	Oh.

They hesitate again.

Gussett	Are you interested in boxing?
Rose	No, not at all.
Gussett	Ah.

Rose	Do you go to the theatre?
Gussett	I went once – about twenty years ago.
Rose	I see.
Gussett	Do you take your holidays in Brighton?
Rose	No, never.
Gussett	Mmm.
Rose	Do you play golf?
Gussett	No, I don't.
Rose	Well, that's not it then.

They hesitate again.

Rose	Do you know, Albert, I don't think we've met before.
Gussett	No, you're right. We haven't.
Rose	Well, er…I'm Harold Rose.
Gussett	And I'm Albert Gussett.
Rose	How do you do?
Gussett	How do you do?

They shake hands.

The passport office

7

This sketch was first performed in 1980. The version given here is very close to the stage version: we have omitted one or two purely visual jokes and a short section addressed to the audience, but apart from those amendments the complete text of the stage version remains intact in this book. This sketch is an example of the type of 'two-person confrontation' which we enjoy very much – the two people being a person having an official function of some kind and a customer, applicant, etc., one or both of whom behave in an unusual way.

Words and expressions

form (n.), *cross…out*; *Where were you born?*
family name, *first name*, *address*, *nationality*

The clerk uses the form-of-address *Miss* before the family name: *Well, Miss Schwarzkopf…* . The use of *Ms* (pronounced /mɪz/ or /məz/), avoiding *Mrs* or *Miss*, is now preferred by many speakers.

The word *Look* is used in the sentence *Look – where do you live?* as a way of being insistent when attempting to make something clear to someone.

Preliminary practice

In this activity, half the students (Students **A**) are travellers who have lost their passports; the other half (Students **B**) are people who have found the passports. Give each Student **A** an identity, i.e. a piece of paper bearing a name, a nationality and an occupation. Some of the details should 'overlap'; for example:

Name: Bill Jones.   *Name: Bill Jones.*
Nationality: British.   *Nationality: American.*
Occupation: Doctor.   *Occupation: Taxi-driver.*

Distribute among Students **B** the corresponding 'passports', i.e. pieces of card, on each of which is written the information from one of the pieces of paper. The students circulate, with Students **B** asking Students **A** *Are you Bill Jones?*, etc., until all the passports have been returned to their owners.

Follow-up activities

① The students could improvise an alternative version of the sketch in groups of four. One student takes the role of the clerk, and sits at a table with a form. This form could simply have the same headings as in the sketch (*Name, Address, Nationality*), or could be expanded to include other headings – some or all of these, for example:

Family name:	Height: ....
First name(s):	Colour of eyes: ....
Date of birth:	Colour of hair: ....
Place of birth:	Address: ....
Nationality:	Telephone number: ....

The other three students independently decide who they are, e.g. a famous contemporary or historical figure. They are then each questioned by the clerk. (The clerk may ask questions in any appropriate way, e.g. *What is your place of birth?* or *Where were you born?*) This is an often amusing activity, as only the individual applicants know their identity in advance.

② For another alternative version, the students (in pairs) could follow the format of the original sketch, but substitute other eccentric reactions to the family name and first name; i.e. instead of using high and low voices, they could sneeze, whistle, cough, make an animal noise, etc. The applicants should not tell the clerks in advance what sounds they are going to use.

Props and costumes

For classroom re-enacting, the following props are useful: a table and two chairs, a sheet of paper (to represent the form), a pen or pencil, pieces of paper (to represent the money), a small notebook (to represent the passport). The clerk could have a pile of notebooks on the table.

A more elaborate performance would require improved versions of the props noted above; it is also useful to have a sign reading 'Passport Office', either on the table or (larger) free-standing on the floor. Regarding costumes: the man should be wearing a raincoat because of the joke which refers to it.

The passport office

Scene A passport office in Britain
Characters The passport office clerk
A man who wants a passport
The man's girl-friend

The clerk is working at her desk. The man comes in and coughs twice.

Clerk Oh, good morning. Can I help you?

Man Yes. Have you got any passports?

Clerk Yes, we have.

Man Oh, good. The shop next door hasn't got any. I'd like twenty, please.

Clerk Twenty?

Man Yes. All different colours.

Clerk I'm sorry. That's impossible.

Man All right. All the *same* colour.

Clerk No, no – it's impossible to have twenty passports.

Man Is it?

Clerk Yes. You can only have one.

Man Oh, all right. One passport, please.

He offers some money.

Clerk Just a minute. It isn't as easy as that. You have to answer some questions.

Man Oh.

Clerk What kind of passport do you want?

Man What kind of passport?

Clerk Yes.

Man A big round yellow one.

Clerk We've only got small blue rectangular ones. When I say 'What kind?', I mean: How long?

Man How long?

Clerk How long? Five years? Ten years?

Man I want it *today*.

Clerk No, I mean: How long do you want it to last?

Man How long do I want it to last?

Clerk Yes.

Man A hundred years.

© Doug Case, Ken Wilson 1995. Published by Heinemann English Language Teaching. This sheet may be photocopied and used within the class.

Clerk	A hundred years?!
Man	Yes.
Clerk	You can't have a passport for a hundred years.
Man	Why not?
Clerk	Er…I don't know. All right – a passport for a hundred years. Now, we have to fill in this form. Er…Do sit down.
Man	Oh, thank you.

He sits down.

Clerk	Now…first question. Name.
Man	William Shakespeare.
Clerk	William Shakespeare?
Man	Yes.
Clerk	Is that your name?
Man	No, but it's a very nice name.
Clerk	Yes, but what's *your* name?
Man	Oh, *my* name. Sorry.
Clerk	Well, what is it?
Man	Smith.
Clerk	(**Writing**) Smith.
Man	(**In a high voice**) That's right. Smith. S-M-I-T-H.
Clerk	Pardon?
Man	Smith, that's right.
Clerk	And what's your first name, Mr Smith?
Man	(**In a high voice**) Charles.
Clerk	Pardon?
Man	Charles.
Clerk	(**Writing**) Charles.
Man	(**In a low voice**) That's right.

The clerk is puzzled.

Clerk	Mr Smith?
Man	(**In a high voice**) Yes?
Clerk	There's something rather strange about the way you speak.
Man	Is there?
Clerk	Yes. When I say your family name –
Man	Smith.
Clerk	Yes, Smith –

Man	(*In a high voice*) Yes?
Clerk	Your voice goes up.
Man	Does it?
Clerk	Yes. And when I say your first name –
Man	Charles.
Clerk	Yes, Charles –
Man	(*In a low voice*) Yes?
Clerk	Your voice goes down.
Man	Er…yes, it's true. It's a very big problem when I'm having a conversation.
Clerk	That's right.
Man	But there *is* a solution.
Clerk	What is it?
Man	You can call me by a different name.
Clerk	A different name?
Man	Yes. Then we can have a normal conversation.
Clerk	Oh, good. What name would you like?
Man	Brunhilde.
Clerk	What?
Man	Call me Brunhilde.
Clerk	Brunhilde –
Man	– Schwarzkopf.
Clerk	I beg your pardon?
Man	Schwarzkopf. Brunhilde Schwarzkopf. Just write it down.
Clerk	(*Suspicious*) Write it down?
Man	Oh, yes – you *must* write it down. You see, if I see my *real* name on a piece of paper, my voice goes funny. (*In a high voice*) Look, there it is –

He taps the form.

Man	(*In a high voice*) – Quick! Smith! Cross it out! Cross it out!
Clerk	Oh. Right.

The clerk crosses out his name.

Man	That's better.
Clerk	(*Writing*) Now…Brunhilde Schwarzkopf. Well, Miss Schwarzkopf, there are one or two more questions. Er…Question two: Address.
Man	Pardon?
Clerk	Address.
Man	No, it isn't.
Clerk	What?

Man   It isn't a dress. I'm not wearing a dress. It's a raincoat.

Clerk   No, no – address, address!

Man   No, no – a raincoat, a raincoat!

Clerk   Look – where do you *live*?

Man   Oh, where do I *live*?

Clerk   Yes.

Man   Round the corner.

Clerk   Can you be more exact?

Man   Er…*just* round the corner.

Clerk   Brunhilde! What is your address?

Man   OK, OK. My address is 14…Brunhilde Street.

Clerk   (***Writing***) 14, Brun – Ah! That means 14 *Smith* Street, doesn't it?

Man   (***In a high voice***) No – 14, *Charles* Street.

Clerk   14, Charles Street.

Man   (***In a low voice***) That's right.

Clerk   Now…nationality.

Man   Er…just write 'British'.

Clerk   *Are* you British?

Man   It doesn't matter. Just write 'British'.

Clerk   Brunhilde, are you or are you not British?

Man   That is a very good question.

Clerk   And what is the answer?

Man   It's a bit complicated.

Clerk   All right, then. Let's start at the beginning. Where were you born?

Man   I don't remember.

Clerk   You don't remember.

Man   No.

Clerk   Why not?

Man   I was very young at the time.

Clerk   Well, what about your father and mother?

Man   They were older than me.

Clerk   Brunhilde! Tell me about your mother.

Man   She was very nice…tall, with a long black beard.

Clerk   Your mother?

Man   Oh no, that was my father…

Clerk   (***Angry***) All right! That's enough! I don't want to hear any more! Just take your passport –

Man   Oh, thank you.

PHOTOCOPIABLE

She gives him a passport.

Clerk   – put a photograph in it, and go anywhere in the world. But *don't* come back here!

She leaves the office.

Man   Hmmm…A British passport, in the name of Brunhilde Schwarzkopf. Excellent. Brunhilde!

His girl-friend, Brunhilde, comes in.

Brunhilde   Ja?

Man   I've got a passport for you.

Brunhilde   Ja?

Man   Now we can go anywhere in the world.

Brunhilde   Ja!

Man   What about a holiday in the sun?

Brunhilde   Ja!

Man   (**To himself**) She doesn't understand a word I say.

Brunhilde   Ja!

© Doug Case, Ken Wilson 1995. Published by Heinemann English Language Teaching. This sheet may be photocopied and used within the class.

Fire practice

8

This sketch was first performed in 1982. In the stage version, the sketch is considerably longer, as the new recruits' fire practice also includes how to get into a house via a door or a window and a certain amount of precarious ladder-practice. The version given here is thus a shortened version, but the sketch resolves in the same way as it does on stage. (Note that the term *fireman* is used in the sketch; this is now usually replaced by the term *fire fighter*, which can be applied to both sexes.)

Words and expressions

Fire Service, fire station, fireman, fire chief, equipment, axe, smash (vb.), *whistle, ambulance, then* (at end of sentence = *in that case*)

Foggins says *Ring, ring* to represent the telephone, because British telephones have a double ringing tone; *Brrrrrr* represents the sound of the dialling tone.

The sketch includes some examples of ellipsis at the start of sentences, typical of colloquial speech: *(I) Don't know, (There's) Nobody there, sir.*

Preliminary practice

This sketch is light-hearted, but of course fire is a very serious subject. The preliminary practice could thus be on the serious side.

You could ask the students to say in English what the regulations are in case of a fire in the school. Pose the question as follows: *What should you do if there's a fire in the school?* The students should give their answers using *you* in the sense of *one* or *everybody*, e.g. *You should leave the school quietly.* (This use of the impersonal 'you' occurs in the sketch.) The students could also give directions for getting from their classroom to the assembly point designated in the event of a fire. They could combine all the information into a fire notice in English (based on one in their language if there is one on display).

Follow-up activities

① As the telephone is used several times in the sketch, the students could follow up with some telephone practice. For example, in threes (Students **A**, **B** and **C**):

A makes a telephone call.
B answers the telephone.
A wants to speak to **C**.
B passes the telephone to **C**.
A then invites **C** to go out (to the cinema, to a party, etc.); they make their arrangements and hang up.

② Here is another activity, which can also be done in threes (Students **X**, **Y** and **Z**).

Firstly, all the **Z**s move to a corner of the room, and remain there for a few moments, so that they do not overhear the following among the **X**s and **Y**s:

X makes a telephone call.
Y answers the telephone.
X wants to speak to **Z**.
Y offers to take a message.
X leaves a short message, saying the reason for the call (which is a question of some kind), and asking for **Z** to call back.
Y notes this message on a piece of paper, and the call is concluded.

The **Y**s then give their written messages to the **Z**s, and the **Z**s call the **X**s back, giving the answers to their questions.

Props and costumes

For classroom re-enacting, these props are useful: a telephone (on a table at the start, and later used by the characters), and a whistle (although the fire chief can simply make the noise vocally).

For a more elaborate performance, you will need: a table, a telephone and whistle, as noted above; an axe (made of wood or stiff cardboard); possibly a small step-ladder, brought on by Boggins and Coggins or already on stage. Note that the telephone has to ring near the beginning and end of the sketch.
Costumes: a uniform for the chief (helmet, heavy jacket, etc.); amusing versions of the uniform for Boggins and Coggins, e.g. slightly too big or too small; the costume for Foggins can be as desired.

Fire practice

Scene   A fire station
Characters   The fire chief

Boggins ⎤
Coggins ⎬ new recruits to the Fire Service
Foggins ⎦

The fire chief is in the fire station. Someone knocks loudly at the door.

Fire chief   Come in!

Foggins comes in.

Foggins   Don't panic!!!

Fire chief   Can I help you?

Foggins   Yes. I want a job.

Fire chief   You want a job.

Foggins   Yes. I want to be a fireman.

Fire chief   You want to be a fireman?

Foggins   That's right.

Fire chief   Why do you want to be a fireman?

Foggins   Well, I like *smashing* things – like doors, and windows, and tables –

Fire chief   Well, I don't know…

Foggins   Please!

Fire chief   What's your name?

Foggins   Foggins.

Fire chief   Foggins?

Foggins   Yeah, 'Smasher' Foggins.

Fire chief   Well, Mr Foggins, do you know anything about the Fire Service? For example, what is the most important thing in a fireman's equipment?

Foggins   What is…the meaning of the word 'equipment'?

Fire chief   Equipment…you know…*things*. What is the most important thing a fireman's got?

Foggins   His axe.

Fire chief   Wrong.

Foggins   What is it, then?

Fire chief   His telephone.

Foggins   His telephone?

Fire chief   Yes, Foggins.

© Doug Case, Ken Wilson 1995. Published by Heinemann English Language Teaching. This sheet may be photocopied and used within the class.

Foggins	You can't smash doors with a telephone.
Fire chief	That's right, Foggins. But when this telephone rings, someone is in trouble. When this telephone rings, someone needs help. When this telephone rings, someone needs the Fire Service.

The telephone rings. The fire chief answers it.

Fire chief	Not now, I'm busy.

He puts down the telephone.

Fire chief	(***To Foggins***) So, Foggins, the most important part of our equipment is –
Foggins	– the telephone.
Fire chief	Right! OK, Foggins, I've got an idea. You can do fire practice today with the new firemen. Would you like to meet them?
Foggins	Yes, please.
Fire chief	Good. Boggins!

Boggins comes in.

Boggins	Sir!
Fire chief	Coggins!

Coggins comes in.

Coggins	Sir!
Fire chief	Foggins, this is Boggins and Coggins. Boggins, Coggins and Foggins. Coggins, Foggins and Boggins. Right – fire practice. Question one. Boggins!
Boggins	Yes, sir!
Fire chief	Where do most fires start?
Boggins	In a box of matches, sir.
Fire chief	No. Coggins?
Coggins	Don't know, sir.
Fire chief	Foggins?
Foggins	What was the question again?
Fire chief	Where do most fires start?
Foggins	At the fire station.
Fire chief	No, Foggins. The answer is: In your house.
Foggins	What?!
Fire chief	Yes, Foggins. In your house.
Foggins	Well, I'm not staying here, then.

Foggins goes towards the door.

Fire chief	Where are you going?

Foggins	I'm going home.
Fire chief	Why?
Foggins	You said most fires start in *my* house.
Fire chief	Not in *your* house, Foggins. In *everybody's* house.

Boggins
Coggins ⎤ What?!
Foggins ⎦

They panic. The fire chief blows his whistle.

Fire chief	Look – don't panic. It's just an expression. It means 'houses in general'.

Boggins
Coggins ⎤ Oh.
Foggins ⎦

Fire chief	Now, question two. Coggins!
Coggins	Sir!
Fire chief	What should you do if there's a fire in your house?
Coggins	Go next door, sir.
Fire chief	No, Coggins. You should call the Fire Service.
Coggins	Ooh, good idea, sir.
Fire chief	And that's where *we* start work. Because the most important part of our equipment is –

Boggins
Coggins ⎤ – the telephone!
Foggins ⎦

Fire chief	Right! Now, telephone practice. Boggins!
Boggins	Sir!
Fire chief	Give the telephone to Coggins.
Boggins	Sir!

Boggins gives the telephone to Coggins.

Fire chief	Coggins!
Coggins	Sir?
Fire chief	*You* are the telephone. Foggins!
Foggins	What?
Fire chief	*You* are the telephone bell.
Foggins	What do you mean?
Fire chief	When I blow my whistle, make a ringing noise. Telephone practice – begin!

The fire chief blows his whistle. Foggins makes a noise like an ambulance.

Fire chief	Not an *ambulance*, Foggins – a telephone! Start again.

The fire chief blows his whistle again.

Foggins	Ring, ring. Ring, ring.
Fire chief	Boggins.
Foggins	Ring, ring.
Boggins	Yes, sir?
Foggins	Ring, ring.
Fire chief	The telephone's ringing.
Foggins	Ring, ring.
Boggins	No, it isn't sir.
Foggins	Ring, ring.
Boggins	It's Foggins, sir. He's going 'Ring, ring', sir.
Foggins	Ring, ring.
Boggins	There you are, sir.
Fire chief	Boggins, answer the telephone!
Foggins	Ring, ring.
Boggins	All right, sir.

Boggins picks up the telephone.

Foggins	Ring, ring. Ring, ring.
Fire chief	Foggins!
Foggins	Ring – What?
Fire chief	Stop it!
Foggins	Brrrrrr.
Boggins	Nobody there, sir.
Fire chief	Let's start again.

Boggins puts down the telephone.

Fire chief	Telephone practice – begin!

The fire chief blows his whistle again.

Foggins	Ring, ring. Ring, ring.

Boggins picks up the telephone.

Boggins	Hello?
Fire chief	Fire station.
Boggins	Oh, hello, fire station!
Fire chief	No, Boggins! You *are* the fire station.
Boggins	Oh, yes. Sorry, sir. Hello? Fire station.

Fire chief	(***In a high voice***) Help! Help!
Boggins	Is something wrong, sir?
Fire chief	No, Boggins. I am an old lady. I'm an old lady, and my house is on fire. That's why I'm calling the fire station.
Boggins	I see, sir.
Fire chief	Continue.
Boggins	Hello, old lady. Can I help you?
Fire chief	(***In a high voice***) Yes. There's a fire in my kitchen.
Boggins	OK. We're on our way.

Boggins puts down the telephone.

Boggins	Was that all right, sir?
Fire chief	Boggins, where is the fire?
Boggins	In the old lady's kitchen, sir.
Fire chief	Where is the old lady's kitchen?
Boggins	In the old lady's house, sir.
Fire chief	Where is the house?
Boggins	Oh, dear!

The telephone rings.

Fire chief	Foggins, stop making that noise.
Foggins	It's not me – it's the telephone.
Fire chief	Is it? Oh, right. Coggins!
Coggins	Sir?
Fire chief	Answer the telephone.
Coggins	Sir!

Coggins answers the telephone.

Coggins	Yes…Yes…Yes…Yes…Yes…Yes. OK, we're on our way.

Coggins puts down the telephone.

Fire chief	Very good, Coggins. What is it?
Coggins	A fire, sir.
Fire chief	Did you get the name?
Coggins	Yes, sir.
Fire chief	Did you get the address?
Coggins	Yes, sir.
Fire chief	Do you know how to get there?
Coggins	Yes, sir.

© Doug Case, Ken Wilson 1995. Published by Heinemann English Language Teaching. This sheet may be photocopied and used within the class.

Fire chief	Right. Get in line and don't panic. This is your first fire. Coggins, where's the fire?
Coggins	In Railway Street, sir.
Fire chief	In Rail – In Railway Street?!
Coggins	Yes, sir.
Fire chief	What number?
Coggins	Number 44, sir.
Fire chief	What?! Quick! Hurry up! Get out of here and *do* something!
Foggins	All right, all right – you said 'Don't panic'.
Fire chief	Never mind 'Don't panic'. Panic!
Boggins	What's the matter, sir? It's just a house on fire.
Fire chief	Yes, but it's *my* house! Panic!

They panic.

© Doug Case, Ken Wilson 1995. Published by Heinemann English Language Teaching. This sheet may be photocopied and used within the class.

9 The post office

This sketch was first performed in 1989, and the version given here is more or less exactly the version we have used in ETT stage shows. On some occasions in stage shows, we have used the name *Watt* for the customer (and her daughter), leading to similar confusions as arise with the traveller in Sketch 12, *The check-in desk*; in the version here, the name used is *Wellington* and the confusion is over the ambiguity in the term 'second name', which may be taken to mean either 'second given name' or 'family name'.

Words and expressions

parcel, post (vb.), *send…by post, coffee-pot, food, look like…, sound like…, smell like…, It's in the book* (= the rule book)

The sketch includes a pun on the words *wait* and *weight*, both of which have the same pronunciation: /weɪt/.

Note the idiomatic use of *he* and *him* to refer to the fish; these pronouns are used rather than *it*, since the fish is a pet and is thus considered almost as a person.

Preliminary practice

Ask the students to each bring a 'parcel'. These 'parcels' should be everyday objects wrapped in paper or in plastic bags. (If the shapes of the parcels give clues to what the objects are, this is fine, although ambiguity is helpful.)

In pairs, the students act out short conversations, with one student being a post office worker and the other a customer. In each pair, the post office worker tries to guess what is in the customer's parcel by saying what it *looks like*; they can also, by handling the parcel or shaking it, say what it *feels like*, *sounds like* or even *smells like*. The customer confirms or denies the guesses, and finally the parcel is opened to reveal the object. Then the roles are reversed to repeat the exercise with the other person's parcel.

Follow-up activities

① The students could devise a sketch of their own, following the general shape of the original, but involving a parcel containing a different unusual object, different details for the person it is being sent to, etc.

② Here is a competitive team-game based around a 'posting box':

Divide the class into six teams, called **A**, **B**, **C**, **D**, **E** and **F**. Each team thinks of five questions* – that is, one question to be put to each of the five other teams – and writes these questions on individual pieces of paper. They then fold the papers in half, and on each paper write the letter of one of the other five teams. All the papers are then 'posted' in a box, and a 'clerk' (yourself, a student, or several students taking turns) is appointed to 'deliver' them, i.e. to dip into the box in front of the whole class, and take out the papers one at a time, saying which team each question is for and reading the question out. The teams are awarded a point for each question correctly answered.

*The questions should be *factual*, and can be about any subjects (although if you wish, they could be limited to a particular subject, e.g. geography, following up the mention of cities in the sketch). They should not be questions which can be answered with a simple *Yes* or *No*. In other words, they should be questions beginning *What…?*, *Who…?*, *How many…?*, etc., or of the type *Name three presidents of the USA*, etc.

Props and costumes

For classroom re-enacting, you will need a table or desk to represent the post office counter, something to represent the fish-shaped parcel and a set of scales (or something to represent it); a small notebook (the 'rule book') and pen or pencil for the clerk are also useful.

For a performance, you will need the counter with the set of scales on it, a sign reading 'Wait here' (e.g. made of wood or cardboard and fixed to a support such as a lampstand), the fish-shaped parcel with a label attached to it, a bag for the customer, and the 'rule book' and pen for the clerk. Costumes: as desired (the clerk doesn't need to wear a uniform of any kind.)

The post office

Scene	A post office in Britain
Characters	The post office clerk
	A customer

The clerk is behind the counter. Some distance from the counter, there is a sign which says 'Wait here'. The customer enters and waits by the sign.

Clerk   Good morning.

The customer does not react.

Clerk   Good morning!

The customer still does not react.

Clerk   Can I help you?

Customer   Pardon?

Clerk   Can I help you?

Customer   I can't hear you!

Clerk   Can I help you?!

Customer   I can't hear you. You're too far away.

Clerk   Well, come over here.

Customer   Pardon?

Clerk   Come over here!!

Customer   Come over there?

Clerk   Yes!!!

Customer   I can't. I've got to wait here.

Clerk   No, you haven't.

Customer   Yes, I have. This sign says 'Wait here'.

Clerk   Yes, but you're the only customer. So you can come over *here*!

Customer   Oh. Right.

The customer goes to the counter.

Clerk   Now…can I help you?

Customer   Can I send a parcel to Australia?

Clerk   Yes, you can.

Customer   Good. I want to send this to my daughter.

The customer produces a large parcel from her bag. The parcel is shaped like a fish.

Clerk	What's this? (**Reading the label on the parcel**) 'Contents: One coffee-pot.' A coffee-pot?
Customer	Yes.
Clerk	It doesn't *look* like a coffee-pot.
Customer	Doesn't it?
Clerk	No.

The clerk bangs the parcel on the counter.

Customer	Be careful!
Clerk	And it doesn't *sound* like a coffee-pot. And…(**Sniffing the parcel**) …it doesn't *smell* like a coffee-pot. It smells like a fish.
Customer	All right, all right, it's a fish.
Clerk	Well, I'm sorry, you can't send a fish by post.
Customer	Why not?
Clerk	Look. It's in the book: 'No food by post.'
Customer	(**Reading from the book**) 'No food by post.' Food?! This isn't food! This is Napoleon!
Clerk	Napoleon?
Customer	Yes, Napoleon. He's my daughter's fish. And my daughter lives in Australia. That's why I want to send him to Australia.
Clerk	Well, you can't send him by post.
Customer	Please!
Clerk	No.
Customer	Please!!
Clerk	Oh, all right. But there's no name on the parcel.
Customer	Oh, sorry. (**She starts writing**) 'Nap-o-le-'
Clerk	Not the name of the *fish*. Your *daughter's* name. What is your daughter's name?
Customer	Josephine.
Clerk	Josephine. And what is her second name?
Customer	Elisabeth.
Clerk	No – when I said 'her *second* name', I meant her *family* name. What is her *family* name?
Customer	It's the same as mine.
Clerk	Yes. But what is it?
Customer	Wellington.
Clerk	Wellington.
Customer	Yes.
Clerk	So…your daughter's name is Josephine Elisabeth Wellington.
Customer	Yes.

Clerk	Address?
Customer	Pardon?
Clerk	Address. Where does she live in Australia?
Customer	Er…
Clerk	Sydney?
Customer	No.
Clerk	Melbourne?
Customer	No.
Clerk	Adelaide?
Customer	Adelaide!
Clerk	Adelaide.
Customer	No. Ah, I remember – Vienna!
Clerk	Vienna?
Customer	Vienna.
Clerk	Vienna's in *Austria*.
Customer	That's what I said.
Clerk	No, you didn't. You said 'Australia'.
Customer	Did I?
Clerk	So this is going to Josephine Wellington in Vienna, Austria.
Customer	Yes. How much is it?
Clerk	That depends on the weight.
Customer	Pardon?
Clerk	Weight.
Customer	Oh. OK.

The customer starts walking back to the 'Wait here' sign.

Clerk	No! I didn't say (**Indicating the sign**) 'wait'. I said (**Indicating the scales on the counter**) 'weight'.

The clerk weighs the parcel.

Clerk	Two and a half kilos. That's £17.50.
Customer	£17.50?! That's very expensive.
Clerk	Well, he *is* going by air.
Customer	By air? Napoleon can't go by air!
Clerk	Why not?
Customer	He's a fish, not a bird.
Clerk	No, he's going on an aeroplane.
Customer	On an aeroplane?

Clerk	Yes.
Customer	How extraordinary! *I'm* going on an aeroplane today.
Clerk	Really?
Customer	Yes. I'm going to visit my daughter.
Clerk	Your daughter Josephine?
Customer	Yes.
Clerk	In Vienna?
Customer	Yes.
Clerk	Well, why don't you take Napoleon with you?
Customer	Take Napoleon with me?
Clerk	Yes. On the aeroplane.
Customer	Take Napoleon with me on the aeroplane?
Clerk	Yes! To Vienna!
Customer	Of course! Take Napoleon with me on the aeroplane to Vienna!
Clerk	Yes!
Customer	And then when I get to Vienna…
Clerk	Yes!!
Customer	…I can post him from there!

The customer picks up the parcel and leaves.

© Doug Case, Ken Wilson 1995. Published by Heinemann English Language Teaching. This sheet may be photocopied and used within the class.

Mr Jones

When someone suggested that we write a sketch illustrating the use of the expressions *So do I, Nor do I,* etc., we hit on the idea of three men who all claimed to be the same person. Why would the three men do this? The answer seemed clear: money! The sketch was first performed in 1975. For this book, the ending has been slightly altered: in the stage version, Mr Jones and his cousin Jane celebrated their good fortune with a song called 'Going to the country', which also involved the *So do I/Nor do I* expressions.

Words and expressions

advertisement, newspaper; celebrate, Congratulations! tax, government, millionaire, share (vb.), *bus fare, What are they called?* (= What are their names?)

Note the ironic tone of *What a coincidence!*, the polite tone of *Sorry to have troubled you*, and the surprised tone of *You've grown up!*

The real Mr Jones, who is from Wales, does not use any specifically Welsh expressions, but he does speak with a slight Welsh accent.

Preliminary practice

Put the students into a circle—or, with a large class, a series of circles—and ask them to say alternately things they like and don't like, building up sequences like this:

Student 1: I like spaghetti.
Student 2: So do I. I don't like snakes.
Student 3: Nor do I. I like playing tennis. (etc.)

Once the pattern is established, the students can vary their statements, saying things they can and can't do, for example, or things they have and haven't got. This will generate varying replies: *So can I/Nor can I, So have I/Nor have I,* etc.

This exercise assumes the students automatically agree. To be able to say what they really think, they will also need to practise responses such as: *Do you? I don't, Don't you? I do,* etc.

Follow-up activities

① The students could think of the situation in the sketch slightly differently, imagining that Mr Jones 2 and Mr Jones 3 are in fact called Charles Edward Jones, but are not the *right* Charles Edward Jones (because they do not come from Cardiff, have more or fewer than three children, none of whom is called Alan, Michael or David). In groups, the students read the sketch again, working out what the two men would have said if they had told the truth. The sketch will remain the same as far as the line *Mine is, too!*, but it will then become clear who is the right Mr Jones. Although in reality she might have stopped earlier, the girl can ask all her questions and all three men can reply. The students should continue up to the point at which Mr Jones 2 and Mr Jones 3 leave.

② In the sketch, Mr Jones 2 and Mr Jones 3 claim that they did not understand the advertisement. They were pretending, but sometimes you *really* need to show that you made a mistake – if you want to return something to a shop, for example, or change a ticket after you've bought it. In pairs, the students could improvise dialogues, based on cue-cards like these:

(For Student A) CLOTHES SHOP: You are the shop assistant.
(For Student B) CLOTHES SHOP: You are a customer. Yesterday you bought a silk shirt by mistake. You wanted a cotton one.

Props and costumes

Simple classroom re-enacting of this sketch requires only three chairs, placed side by side. (We have found that it works best to seat the real Mr Jones between the two other men, rather than at one end.)

For a more elaborate performance, the following props are useful: a newspaper for each of the three men; a pen and a clipboard with some papers on it for the girl. Costumes can be as desired: it is not necessary for the men to wear anything distinctively Welsh; the girl may like to wear a pair of sober glasses to give her a stern official appearance in the early part of the sketch.

Mr Jones

Scene   An office, at four o'clock one afternoon
Characters   A girl
Mr Charles Jones
A second 'Mr Jones'
A third 'Mr Jones'

Mr Jones goes into an office.

Mr Jones   Good afternoon.

Girl   Good afternoon.

Mr Jones   My name's Jones. Charles Jones. I come from Wales, from Cardiff. I saw an advertisement in the newspaper. It said: 'Charles Jones. Money. Four o'clock. Tuesday afternoon.' And it gave this address.

Girl   Ah yes. Wait in here please, Mr Jones.

She takes Mr Jones into another office.

Mr Jones   Thank you.

Girl   With these two gentlemen.

Mr Jones   Oh, thank you.

The girl goes out.

Mr Jones   Good afternoon.

Mr Jones 2   Good afternoon.

Mr Jones   Good afternoon.

Mr Jones 3   Good afternoon.

Mr Jones   Nice day, isn't it?

Mr Jones 2   Yes.

Mr Jones 3   Yes, it is.

The girl comes in.

Girl   Now – Mr Jones?

Mr Jones
Mr Jones 2   ⎱ Yes?
Mr Jones 3

Girl   Mr *Jones*.

Mr Jones
Mr Jones 2   ⎱ Yes?
Mr Jones 3

Girl	Which one of you is Mr Jones?
Mr Jones	I am.
Mr Jones 2	So am I.
Mr Jones 3	So am I.
Mr Jones	No, *my* name's Jones.
Mr Jones 2	So's mine.
Mr Jones 3	So's mine.
Girl	I want to speak to Mr *Charles* Jones.
Mr Jones	Charles Jones! That's me!
Mr Jones 2	No, *I'm* Charles Jones.
Mr Jones 3	That's my name, too!
Girl	Charles *Edward* Jones.
Mr Jones	Yes! My name is Charles Edward Jones.
Mr Jones 3	So's mine.
Mr Jones 2	Mine is, too!
Girl	I want to speak to Mr Charles Edward Jones from Cardiff.
Mr Jones	That's right. *I* come from Cardiff.
Mr Jones 2	So do I.
Mr Jones 3	So do I.
Girl	The Mr Jones I want to see has got three children.
Mr Jones	Yes, that's me! I've got three children.
Mr Jones 3	So have I.

The other man hesitates.

Girl	What about you?
Mr Jones 2	I've got three children.
Mr Jones	You haven't! What are they called?
Mr Jones 2	What are *yours* called?
Mr Jones	Alan, Michael and David.
Mr Jones 2	So are mine.
Mr Jones 3	What a coincidence! So are mine.
Girl	So you *all* say you're Mr Jones?
Mr Jones **Mr Jones 2** **Mr Jones 3**	Yes.
Girl	And you *all* saw the advertisement in the newspaper.
Mr Jones **Mr Jones 2** **Mr Jones 3**	Yes.

Girl	(**Very seriously**) Well, Mr Charles Edward Jones, who lives in Cardiff, and has three children, hasn't paid any tax for the last five years. He must pay the government *five thousand pounds.*
Mr Jones 2	Er…actually, my name *isn't* Jones.
Mr Jones 3	Nor is mine, and I don't live in Cardiff, either.
Mr Jones 2	Nor do I. I live in…Edinburgh, as a matter of fact. I didn't understand the advertisement.
Mr Jones 3	Nor did I. I didn't realize it meant Charles *Edward* Jones.
Mr Jones 2	Nor did I. My name isn't Charles Edward Jones.
Mr Jones 3	Nor is mine. *He's* the man you're looking for.
Mr Jones	Oh dear.
Mr Jones 2	Yes, of course he is! Sorry to have troubled you. Goodbye.
Mr Jones 3	Yes, sorry to have troubled you. Goodbye.

The two men leave.

Girl	So you're Mr Jones.
Mr Jones	Yes.
Girl	Congratulations!
Mr Jones	Eh?
Girl	You're a rich man.
Mr Jones	I'm not!
Girl	Yes, you are. You've got a lot of money!
Mr Jones	I haven't. I can't pay that tax.
Girl	There isn't any tax!
Mr Jones	I haven't got – No tax?
Girl	No. That was just a story. I had to find the *real* Mr Jones.
Mr Jones	Why?
Girl	Because the real Mr Jones is a very rich man.
Mr Jones	I don't understand.
Girl	Mr Jones – Charlie – Your great-uncle Max died last week.
Mr Jones	Oh, no…
Girl	And his money goes to you!
Mr Jones	To me? But great-uncle Max was a millionaire!
Girl	That's right.
Mr Jones	So now *I'm* a millionaire?
Girl	Er…no.
Mr Jones	Oh.
Girl	You're *half* a millionaire.

© Doug Case, Ken Wilson 1995. Published by Heinemann English Language Teaching. This sheet may be photocopied and used within the class.

Mr Jones   Half a millionaire? Which half? The top half or the bottom half?

Girl   No, no, no. You share the money with one other relation.

Mr Jones   Half a millionaire! Who do I share the money with?

Girl   Me!

Mr Jones   You?

Girl   Yes, I'm your cousin Jane.

Mr Jones   Cousin Jane? Really? *You've* grown up!

Girl   So have you.

Mr Jones   And now you're half a millionaire.

Girl   And so are you! Let's go out and celebrate.

Mr Jones   Good idea! Let's go out and celebrate! Come on!

He opens the door.

Mr Jones   Oh…er…Jane?

Girl   Yes?

Mr Jones   Have you got enough money for the bus fare?

11 The shoe stall

This sketch was first performed in 1990; we had previously written several sketches set in shops, and thought that a market stall would also be a promising comic situation. In the stage version of the sketch, on the line 'This is a pear', Harry produces from his case a card showing a picture of a pear, and follows it up with two other cards ('This is an apple', 'And this is a banana'); his multiple-choice questions ('Are you (A) Unhappy?', etc.) are also on cards which he produces from his case.

Words and expressions

What's the problem?, complain, make a complaint, take (something) seriously, husband, similar, owe

The sketch includes a pun on the words *pair* and *pear*, both of which are pronounced: /peə[r]/.

A number of adjectives describing feelings occur in the sketch: *satisfied, unhappy, annoyed, angry, furious, suicidal*; there are also several intensifiers: *very, extremely, absolutely, completely.*

Preliminary practice

Here is a lively competitive game which practises adjectives expressing feelings (negative ones like those in the sketch – *angry, furious,* etc. – and more positive ones such as *surprised, delighted,* etc.):

Divide the class into two teams. A volunteer from each team sits in a chair with their back to the board. The remaining members of each team then choose an adjective and write it on the board behind the *other* team's volunteer. The adjectives are now mimed by the teams. So, for example, Team **A** choose the adjective *angry* and write it on the board behind Team **B**'s volunteer, and the remaining members of Team **B** mime it. At the same time, Team **A** mime the adjective chosen by Team **B**. Each of the two volunteers tries to be the first to guess their adjective correctly.

Follow-up activities

① The students could improvise some short sketches between a stallholder and a customer, in a similar format to that of the original sketch, i.e. the customers are bringing something back to make a complaint about it, and the stallholder is unwilling to admit that there is a problem. Cue-cards may be helpful for this activity. Those for the stallholders should all read:

You work in a market. You sold something to a customer. A relative or friend of the customer is coming back to complain about it. Don't accept the complaint immediately.

And here are some possibilities for the customers:

Your mother bought an umbrella in the market yesterday. It has holes in it. Complain to the stallholder.
Your sister bought a radio in the market last Friday. It only gets one station. Complain to the stallholder.
Your father bought a shirt in the market last week. It has shrunk in the washing-machine. Complain to the stallholder.
Your brother bought a book in the market yesterday. The last page is missing. Complain to the stallholder.

② Alternatively, the students could simply practise in pairs some more straightforward conversations between a stallholder and a customer: having decided what the stallholder is selling, they improvise choosing something to buy, discussing the price, etc.

Props and costumes

For classroom re-enacting, you will need a table to represent the stall, two pairs of shoes of different colours, and some pieces of paper to represent the money.

For a performance, you could cover a table with a cloth to represent the stall. Harry needs a hat with a small card reading 'Honest Harry' fixed to it; a case containing one red shoe and one green shoe, and a pear (e.g. in his pocket). The customer needs a shopping-bag in which there is a shoe box containing one red shoe and one green shoe. Both Harry and the customer need some paper money. You may also like to incorporate the cards mentioned in the introductory note above.

The shoe stall

Scene A shoe stall in a street-market in Britain
Characters Honest Harry, the stallholder
A customer

The stallholder is standing at his stall; he has a small card in his hat, saying 'Honest Harry'. The customer comes to the stall, carrying a shoe-box.

Harry Good morning, madam. Can I help you?

Customer Are you Honest Harry?

Harry Er…maybe. Why?

Customer I want to make a complaint to Honest Harry.

Harry A complaint?

Customer Yes.

Harry In that case, I'm not Honest Harry.

Customer What?

Harry Honest Harry's on holiday.

Customer Oh. (**Noticing the card in his hat**) Wait a minute – your *hat* says 'Honest Harry'.

Harry Oh, yes – this is Honest Harry's hat. I'm wearing it while he's on holiday.

Customer What?!

Harry I'll tell you what I'll do. I'll give you Harry's telephone number…in Argentina.

Customer Now listen to me –

Harry All right, all right, all right. I *am* Honest Harry. What's the problem?

The customer puts the shoe-box on the stall.

Customer Well, my husband came here yesterday.

Harry Oh, really?

Customer Yes. And he bought these shoes.

The customer takes two shoes from the box (one is red, the other is green) and closes it.

Harry Yes?

Customer Well, my husband can't wear these.

Harry Why not? Are they too big?

Customer No.

Harry Too small?

Customer No.

Harry	So what's the problem?
Customer	They're not the same colour.
Harry	Not the same colour?
Customer	That's right.
Harry	Not the same colour as what?
Customer	They're not the same colour as each other! One of them's red and the other one's green.
Harry	Oh, yes! One of them's red and the other one's green.
Customer	Yes!
Harry	I see! So which one are you complaining about?
Customer	Pardon?
Harry	Which one don't you like?
Customer	Look, there's nothing wrong with the shoes –
Harry	Good.
Customer	– but they're not a pair.
Harry	No, you're right, madam. They're not a pear. *This* is a pear.

Harry produces a pear and bites it.

Harry	Mmm, delicious!
Customer	I don't think you're taking this very seriously.
Harry	Sorry, madam. Let's start at the beginning. Your husband bought these shoes.
Customer	Yes.
Harry	From me.
Customer	Yes.
Harry	And you're not satisfied with them.
Customer	That's right. I'm not satisfied at all.
Harry	What do you mean, exactly?
Customer	What do you mean: 'What do I mean'?
Harry	What do I mean what do you mean?
Customer	Yes.
Harry	What I mean is this: Are you: (A) 'Unhappy', (B) 'Annoyed', (C) 'Angry', or (D) 'Suicidal'?
Customer	Well, I'm unhappy.
Harry	You're unhappy.
Customer	Yes.
Harry	You're not annoyed.
Customer	No – well, yes, I am.
Harry	So you're annoyed.

© Doug Case, Ken Wilson 1995. Published by Heinemann English Language Teaching. This sheet may be photocopied and used within the class.

Customer	Yes.
Harry	You're not just unhappy – you're annoyed.
Customer	Yes.
Harry	But you're not angry.
Customer	No.
Harry	You're sure?
Customer	Yes.
Harry	Oh, you *are* angry.
Customer	No! I'm *sure* I'm *not angry!*
Harry	You're not angry.
Customer	I'm not angry!
Harry	Well, you look angry to me.
Customer	All right, I'm angry!!
Harry	You're angry! Right. But not suicidal.
Customer	That's right.
Harry	Good. You're angry!
Customer	Yes!!
Harry	Now, are you: (A) 'Very angry', (B) 'Very very angry', (C) 'Extremely angry', or (D) 'Absolutely furious'?
Customer	Look, this is stupid.
Harry	Oh, it's stupid, is it?
Customer	Yes, it's stupid.
Harry	I see. Would you say it's: (A) 'Very stupid', (B) 'Very very stupid', (C) 'Completely stupid', or (D) 'Absolutely idiotic'?
Customer	Look, all I want to do is change these shoes.
Harry	Change the shoes? Well, why didn't you say so? You're very lucky, madam, because I have here another pair of shoes that are very similar.

Harry produces the corresponding red shoe and green shoe, and puts them on the stall.

Customer	No, wait a minute – that's a red one and a green one as well.
Harry	You're quite right. OK, let me change this red one for this green one.

He does so, making a red pair and a green pair.

Customer	Thank you.
Harry	And this green one for this red one.

He does so, making two mixed pairs again.

Harry	Satisfied?
Customer	No.

Harry	All right then. I'll change this green one for this red one…

He does so, making a red pair and a green pair.

Harry	…and this red one for this green one.

He does so, making two mixed pairs again.

Customer	Look –
Harry	Just a minute – I've got a better idea. Your husband bought *this* pair of shoes…

He indicates one mixed pair.

Harry	…so if you buy *this* pair as well…

He indicates the other mixed pair.

Customer	Yes?
Harry	…you can have one pair, and your husband can have the other.
Customer	All right. (**Putting the two pairs into her bag**) One pair…two pairs. How much is that?
Harry	Twenty pounds.
Customer	Twenty pounds. (**Giving Harry a £20 note**) Here you are.
Harry	No – it's twenty pounds a *pair*. That's forty pounds.
Customer	Forty pounds?
Harry	Yes.
Customer	But my husband paid you twenty pounds yesterday.
Harry	Did he?
Customer	Yes. So *you* owe *me* twenty pounds.
Harry	(**Confused**) Do I?
Customer	Yes.
Harry	Oh. (**Giving back the £20 note**) Here you are then.
Customer	Thank you. Goodbye.

The customer leaves.

Harry	Goodbye. (**Realizing his mistake**) Er….no…just a minute…Come back!

He runs after the customer.

© Doug Case, Ken Wilson 1995. Published by Heinemann English Language Teaching. This sheet may be photocopied and used within the class.

The check-in desk

12

An early version of this sketch was performed in 1984, but it was considerably revised in 1993, and that is the version given here. We have omitted one or two mainly visual sections from the stage version: a joke based on the term *hand luggage* (the traveller has a shoulder-bag shaped like a large hand), and a sequence in which the clerk gives the traveller instructions supposedly to take him to another check-in desk – via a long (off-stage) detour 'up the stairs', 'along the corridor', etc. – but which in fact finally bring him back to the same desk.

Words and expressions

Connected with air travel:
airport, airline, (aero)plane, passenger, pilot, captain, luggage, seat, seatbelt, (non-) smoking, departure gate, fly, flight, Have a good flight!

Connected with food:
chicken, carrot, meal, vegetarian (n.)

The sketch includes puns on the name *Watt* and the word *what*, both pronounced /wɒt/; and on the words *right* and *write*, both pronounced /raɪt/.

Preliminary practice

Put the class into groups of three or four, and ask the groups to write down as many questions as they can think of which would be asked by a check-in clerk at an airport. Walk round replying to any queries the groups may have about vocabulary. The groups then share with the whole class the questions they have noted down, and points may be awarded to groups who have questions which no other group thought of.

Then ask the groups to think of completely *irrelevant* questions to ask someone who is checking in at an airport: for example, *What is your favourite pop group?, Have you ever visited a museum?* The groups then offer their irrelevant questions to the class; if other groups can find a way to make the questions relevant, *they* – rather than the questioners – gain points.

Follow-up activities

① In the sketch, the check-in clerk gives reasons for the name *Elephant Airlines*: the planes are very big, move very slowly, and make a noise like an elephant. Here is an activity based on that idea.

Divide the class into small groups. Each group thinks of a name for an airline, and of a reason or reasons for the name. They write the names on pieces of paper, which are then collected and put into a hat or a box, or simply in a pile. Students pick up the pieces of paper one at a time, reading out the name of the airline on each one and asking *Why is it called (…) Airlines?* The group who invented the name give their reason(s), and other groups can suggest reasons too.

② Here is another group activity. The situation is a plane, on which the intercom has broken down, and the pilots and stewards all have sore throats and cannot speak; information must therefore be given to the passengers in mime. Each group is given an announcement written on a piece of paper: for example

Ladies and gentlemen, we are flying at 35,000 feet.
We will soon be serving dinner and drinks.
We will shortly be landing at London Airport.
Please do not smoke when moving about in the cabin.
The weather in London is cold, wet and windy.

The groups decide how they can mime their information. Each group then does so and the other groups try to deduce the meaning of the mimes.

Props and costumes

For classroom re-enacting, you will need a table or desk to represent the check-in desk, a chair, a small bag for the traveller's hand luggage, and a piece of paper to represent the ticket; it is also useful to have a belt, and something to represent the plastic chicken and the large carrot (e.g. pictures thereof).

For a performance, improved versions of those props will be required, and it is useful if the table or lectern used for the check-in desk has a large sign on the front reading 'Elephant Airlines'. Costumes: airline uniform for the clerk; perhaps holiday clothes for the traveller; pilot's uniform for Captain Strange.

The check-in desk

Scene   The 'Elephant Airlines' check-in desk at an international airport in Britain

Characters   The check-in clerk
An English traveller
Captain Strange, a pilot

The traveller comes to the check-in desk. He is carrying just one small bag, as hand luggage.

Clerk   Good morning, sir. Can I help you?

Traveller   Monte Carlo!

Clerk   Pardon?

Traveller   Monte Carlo!

Clerk   Oh! Hello, Mr Carlo.

Traveller   No! I want to *fly* to *Monte Carlo*.

Clerk   Oh, I see!

Traveller   Can I check in here?

Clerk   For the flight to Monte Carlo?

Traveller   Yes.

Clerk   Who are you flying with?

Traveller   Pardon?

Clerk   Who are you flying with?

Traveller   Nobody – I'm going by myself.

Clerk   No, sir. I mean, which *airline* are you flying with?

Traveller   Oh. Elephant Airlines. Here's my ticket.

Clerk   Thank you.

Traveller   This is my first flight, you know.

Clerk   Well, I'm sure you'll enjoy it, sir. (**Reading from the ticket**) Elephant Airlines, Flight 999 to Monte Carlo.

Traveller   Er…Why is it called 'Elephant Airlines'?

Clerk   Well, sir, the planes are very big –

Traveller   (**Pleased**) Ah.

Clerk   They move very slowly –

Traveller   (**Uneasy**) Ah.

Clerk   And they make a strange noise.

Traveller   A strange noise?

Clerk	Yes. A noise like an elephant.

The clerk makes an elephant noise.

Traveller	What?! Your planes sound like elephants?!
Clerk	Yes, sir.
Traveller	But – But – But –
Clerk	Take it easy, sir. They're quite safe. Now... (**Reading from the ticket**) ...Mr Right.
Traveller	Pardon?
Clerk	Mr Right.
Traveller	No, that's wrong.
Clerk	Pardon?
Traveller	My name isn't Right. It's wrong.
Clerk	Your name is Wrong?
Traveller	Yes.
Clerk	Well, Mr Wrong –
Traveller	No! My name isn't right on the ticket.
Clerk	Yes, it is. Look...Mr Right.
Traveller	No...my *name isn't* Right!
Clerk	Ah! Your name isn't Right!
Traveller	Right!
Clerk	Right! What is your name?
Traveller	Watt.
Clerk	Your name.
Traveller	Watt!
Clerk	What is your name?!
Traveller	Yes! Watt *is* my name!!
Clerk	Ah! Right!
Traveller	No! Watt!
Clerk	Right! Watt!
Traveller	Yes. (**Pointing at the ticket**) Write Watt!

The clerk corrects his name on the ticket.

Clerk	Right. Any luggage, Mr Watt?
Traveller	Pardon?
Clerk	Have you got any luggage?
Traveller	Just this little bag.
Clerk	That's fine. Now, smoking or non-smoking?
Traveller	Non-smoking, please.

Clerk	Eating or non-eating?
Traveller	Pardon?
Clerk	Eating or non-eating? Do you want a meal on the plane?
Traveller	Oh. Yes, please.
Clerk	Er…Here you are.

The clerk produces a plastic chicken.

Traveller	What's that?!
Clerk	Your lunch.
Traveller	But that's a chicken.
Clerk	Yes.
Traveller	I can't eat that. I'm a vegetarian!
Clerk	Oh. Well, in that case…er…you can have this carrot.

The clerk gives the traveller a large carrot.

Traveller	(**Confused**) Thank you.
Clerk	Well, everything seems to be in order. So…your seat.
Traveller	Yes.
Clerk	Where is it?
Traveller	Pardon?
Clerk	Where's your seat?
Traveller	My seat?
Clerk	Yes. Have you got one?
Traveller	Aren't there any seats on the plane?
Clerk	(**Laughing**) Seats…on the plane?
Traveller	Yes.
Clerk	No. You have to take your own.
Traveller	I haven't got a seat.
Clerk	No seat?
Traveller	No.
Clerk	You've come to the airport without a seat?
Traveller	Well, it *is* my first flight…
Clerk	Well, never mind – you can borrow mine.

The clerk gives the traveller her chair.

Traveller	But wait a minute, this isn't an aeroplane seat, is it?
Clerk	Well, it's a seat – you put it on an aeroplane – it's an aeroplane seat.
Traveller	What about a seatbelt?

Clerk	Here you are.

The clerk produces a belt.

Traveller	Look – that isn't a seatbelt, is it?
Clerk	It's a belt – (**Putting it on the seat**) you put it on a seat – it's a seatbelt.
Traveller	Thank you. Is that everything?
Clerk	Yes, sir. You've got your seat, you've got your seatbelt, and you've got your carrot.
Traveller	Where do I go now?
Clerk	To the Departure Gate.
Traveller	The Departure Gate.
Clerk	Yes. Gate Number 13.
Traveller	Thank you.
Clerk	Have a good flight, sir.
Traveller	(**Still confused**) Thank you.

The traveller starts to leave. The clerk bursts out laughing.

Traveller	What's the matter?
Clerk	I'm sorry, sir. You didn't believe all that, did you?
Traveller	All what?
Clerk	All that about the seat – and the seatbelt – and the carrot.
Traveller	What do you mean?
Clerk	Sir…it was all a joke.
Traveller	A joke?
Clerk	Yes. You see, *you* are the one-millionth passenger to fly with Elephant Airlines, so we thought we'd have a bit of fun!
Traveller	Oh! So it's not true: the seat, the seatbelt – and the carrot!
Clerk	No, sir – flying isn't like that!
Traveller	I thought it was a bit strange!
Clerk	Yes.
Traveller	But this *is* my first flight.
Clerk	Yes.
Traveller	You must think I'm a complete idiot!
Clerk	Yes. Anyway, you're the one-millionth passenger, so the captain himself is going to accompany you to the plane.
Traveller	The captain? You mean the pilot himself?
Clerk	That's right, sir.
Traveller	Wonderful!
Clerk	I'll call him. Captain Strange!

Captain Strange enters, singing 'Flying, up above the clouds'. He is rather strange.

Traveller Is *that* the captain?

Clerk Yes, sir. Captain Strange is the *best* pilot with Elephant Airlines. In fact, he's the *only* pilot with Elephant Airlines. Er…Captain Strange!

Captain Yes?

Clerk This is Mr Watt, your very special passenger for today's flight.

Captain Mr Watt! How nice to meet you! How very, very nice!

Clerk You go with the captain, Mr Watt. He'll take you to the plane.

Captain The plane, yes. Where is it?

Traveller What?!

Captain The plane.

Traveller *I* don't know!

Clerk It's at Departure Gate 13, Captain.

Captain Thank you. Tell me, Mr Watt…Have you ever flown a plane before?

Traveller No. Why?

Captain Well, I'm not feeling very well. I thought that perhaps *you* could fly the plane.

Traveller What?!

Captain Take it easy, Mr Watt. Flying a plane is no problem.

Traveller But –

Captain Come on, Mr Watt. Let's go.

Traveller Aaargh!

The traveller leaves, accompanied by Captain Strange, singing 'Flying, up above the clouds'.

Clerk Have a good flight, sir!

This sketch was first performed in 1990. We are quite fond of sketches involving groups of people in uniform, since they provide good scope for humour when dignity and efficiency are aimed for but not achieved. Apart from this sketch, for example, we have used sketches involving customs officers, astronauts, and – included in this book – the fire brigade (Sketch 8) and (in Book 2) the army (Sketch 2). (Note that some regional police forces in Britain use the term *WPC (Woman Police Constable)* as in this sketch; others use *PC (Police Constable)* for both sexes.)

Words and expressions

Connected with the police:
inspector, constable, police force, criminal, arrest, equipment, whistle, truncheon, notebook, pen

Clothes vocabulary:
clothes, uniform, hat, helmet, blouse, shirt, trousers, skirt, boots

The sketch includes a pun on the two senses of the word *left*: as the opposite of 'right', and in the expression *There won't be any criminals left.*

Preliminary practice

When the police are at training college, they often observe crimes being acted out by professional actors and then comment on what they saw. A version of this activity can serve as a warm-up to this sketch.

Divide the class into groups of five or six, and ask each group to act out a crime, such as a bank robbery or the theft of a car. In each group, some students will be the 'perpetrators' and the others will be the 'victims'. Give the groups some time to prepare, and while they are doing this go round ensuring that they are not simply going to *mime* the event, but also *speak* during it. The groups then act out their 'crimes' for the rest of the class to watch. After each 'crime', the rest of the class say what they can remember about it, including who did what, what was said, etc.

Follow-up activities

① The sketch includes various interpretations of the abbreviations *PC* and *WPC,* some more plausible than others. You could base an activity which requires the students to do some inventive quick-thinking on some other abbreviations, like this, for example:

Write some English abbreviations on small pieces of paper. These could be abbreviations such as *BBC* (British Broadcasting Corporation), *CIA* (Central Intelligence Agency), *FBI* (Federal Bureau of Investigation), *GB* (Great Britain), *ITV* (Independent Television), *LA* (Los Angeles), *NATO* (North Atlantic Treaty Organisation), *OPEC* (Organisation of Petroleum Exporting Countries), *RAF* (Royal Air Force), *UK* (United Kingdom), *UN* (United Nations), *WHO* (World Health Organisation), etc., or any you feel suitable. In turns, the students take a piece of paper, read out the abbreviation written on it, and invent a meaning for the abbreviation. (These meanings can be as fanciful as they like; for example, 'Brazilian Banana Company' or 'Bring big cheques' for *BBC*.) The other students then give the real meaning.

② You could base an activity on the 'notebook' idea from the sketch. Each student writes a sentence on a piece of paper – something personal (but not intimate or embarrassing) about themselves. These sentences are then collected and read out, with the students trying to guess who wrote each one.

Props and costumes

For classroom re-enacting, the following props are useful: three whistles, for Black, Green and Brown (although they can make the noises vocally if no whistles are available); two truncheons (or something to represent them, e.g. rolled paper), for Brown and Green; a children's comic (or magazine to represent it) for Grey; a small notebook, for Brown; and a pen, for Black.

For a performance, real versions of those props will be needed, plus costumes for the characters: an inspector's uniform for Black; helmet, shirt, trousers and boots for Green; hat, blouse, skirt and boots for Brown; helmet, boots, bright shirt, long shorts for Grey.

The police

Scene   A public meeting at which Inspector Black is giving a talk about the British police force
Characters   Inspector Black
PC Green
WPC Brown
PC Grey

Black   Good evening, ladies and gentlemen. My name is Inspector Black, and I've come here tonight to talk to you about the police force in Great Britain. The police force in Great Britain is very professional, very intelligent and very…professional. So, I'd like you to meet some of my very professional and intelligent police officers. First of all, I'd like you to meet PC Green. Ladies and gentlemen, PC Green.

PC Green enters.

Black   Good evening, PC Green.

Green   Good evening, Inspector Black.

Black   Now, what does PC mean? Tell them, Green.

Green   I beg your pardon, Inspector?

Black   Tell them.

Green   Tell them what, Inspector?

Black   What do the letters 'PC' stand for?

Green   Oh! 'PC' stands for 'Peter Christopher'.

Black   What?

Green   It's my name, Inspector. Peter Christopher Green – PC Green.

Black   Green…

Green   Yes, Inspector?

Black   Do you think that we call you 'PC Green' because your name is Peter Christopher Green?

Green   Yes, Inspector.

Black   Well, you're wrong. 'PC' stands for something else.

Green   Really?

Black   Yes. Now think: What does 'PC' stand for?

Green   Postcard?

Black   No!

Green   Personal computer?

Black   No!!

Green   Oh, I know! Prince Charles!

© Doug Case, Ken Wilson 1995. Published by Heinemann English Language Teaching. This sheet may be photocopied and used within the class.

Black   Green, 'PC' does not mean 'Prince Charles', or 'postcard', or 'personal computer'. It means 'Police Constable'!

Green   Really? I didn't know that.

Black   You are Police Constable Green.

Green   Thank you, Inspector.

Black   Now, ladies and gentlemen, I'd like you to meet another British police officer: WPC Brown.

WPC Brown enters.

Brown   Hello.

Black   Now, if 'PC' means 'Police Constable', what does 'WPC' mean?

Brown   'Wife of Police Constable.'

Black   Don't be stupid, Brown! You are not 'Wife of Police Constable'!

Brown   Yes, I am, Inspector. I'm married to PC Green.

Green   That's right, sir. We're very happy.

Black   'WPC' means 'Woman Police Constable'. Now, ladies and gentlemen, as you can see, Green and Brown are wearing nice blue and white uniforms.

Green and Brown demonstrate their uniforms like fashion models.

Black   Hat – or helmet. Blouse – or shirt. Skirt – or trousers. Boots…or boots. So, this is a police uniform. But there are a lot of police officers out there in the street with no uniform.

Green   No uniform?!

Brown   They must be very cold, Inspector.

Black   No! They're wearing normal clothes.

Brown   Why's that, Inspector?

Black   They're wearing normal clothes because they want to look like normal people. So…here is a police officer dressed exactly like a normal person. Ladies and gentlemen, PC Grey.

PC Grey enters. He is wearing a police helmet and boots, and a pair of long shorts and a brightly-coloured shirt.

Black   Now, as you can see, there is no way that you would know that PC Grey is a police officer.

Brown   Except for the helmet.

Black   Except for the helmet.

Green   And the boots.

Black   And the boots. Except for the helmet and the boots, there is no way that you would know that Police Constable Grey is a police officer.

PC Grey does not look very pleased.

Black   Now, Grey – tell these people what it feels like to be a police officer with no uniform.

Grey   It feels stupid.

Black   What?

Grey   It feels stupid. I mean, I'm a police officer: I want to wear a uniform!

Black	That's enough, Grey.
Grey	I don't want to walk the streets looking like this!
Black	Grey! Get back in line!
Grey	Would *you* walk the streets looking like this?

The Inspector blows his whistle. Grey gets back in line.

Black	Green! Brown! Grey! It's time for equipment demonstration.
Green **Brown** **Grey**	Equipment demonstration!
Black	Now, every police officer has three important pieces of equipment. A whistle –

Green produces a whistle.

Black	– a truncheon –

Brown produces a truncheon.

Black	– and a notebook.

Grey produces a comic.

Black	A notebook, Grey, not a comic.
Grey	They didn't give me a notebook.
Black	I see.
Grey	No uniform, no notebook. It's ridiculous!

The Inspector blows his whistle.

Black	That's enough, Grey! Now, what are these very important pieces of equipment for? First of all, the whistle. The whistle is used to attract the attention of other police officers. Like this:

Green blows his whistle.

Green	Oi!

Brown blows her whistle.

Brown	Oi!

Grey has no whistle.

Grey	No uniform, no notebook – and no whistle!
Black	And now, the truncheon. Green, Brown, Grey – ready with your truncheons!
Green	Sir!
Brown	Sir!

Grey has no truncheon.

© Doug Case, Ken Wilson 1995. Published by Heinemann English Language Teaching. This sheet may be photocopied and used within the class.

Grey	No uniform, no notebook, no whistle – and no truncheon!

The Inspector blows his whistle.

Black	Right – forget the truncheons. The notebook. Green?
Green	Yes, Inspector?
Black	What is the notebook for?
Green	For making notes, Inspector.
Black	Very good, Green. Brown?
Brown	Yes, Inspector?
Black	Have you got anything in your notebook?
Brown	Yes, Inspector.
Black	Good. Read it.
Brown	Oh. All right. (***Reading***) ' "What I did today", by Woman Police Constable Brown, aged twenty-five…and a half. Got up. Said "Hello" to Police Constable Green. Made a cup of coffee –'
Black	Thank you, Brown. Grey?
Grey	Yes, Inspector?
Black	Have *you* got anything in *your* notebook?
Grey	(***Holding up the comic***) You mean this?
Black	Yes.
Grey	Yes. (***Reading***) ' "Mickey Mouse goes for a picnic." On Saturday, Mickey and his friends –'
Black	Grey! I mean: Have you *written* anything in it?
Grey	No.
Black	Why not?
Grey	Because they didn't give me a pen!!
Black	All right, all right, all right. Here you are.

The Inspector gives Grey a pen.

Grey	Thank you, Inspector.
Black	Now, have you all got everything you need? Whistle?
Green	Yes!
Brown	Yes!
Grey	No!
Black	Truncheon?
Green	Yes!
Brown	Yes!
Grey	No!
Black	Notebook?
Green	Yes!

Brown	Yes!
Grey	No!
Black	Boots?
Green	Yes!
Brown	Yes!
Grey	Yes!
Black	Helmet?
Green	Yes!
Brown	No!
Grey	Yes!
Black	(**Slightly confused**) Well, that seems all right. Now it's time for action!
Green **Brown** **Grey**	Action! Right!
Black	I want you to get out there, in the street!
Green **Brown** **Grey**	In the street! Right!
Black	And find some criminals!
Green **Brown** **Grey**	Criminals! Right!
Black	And when you find them…
Green **Brown** **Grey**	Right!
Black	You know what to do!
Green **Brown** **Grey**	What?
Black	You arrest them!
Green **Brown** **Grey**	Arrest them! Right!
Black	And then there won't be any criminals left!
Green **Brown** **Grey**	Right!
All	Left! Right! Left! Right! Left! Right!…

They all march away.

Hotel Splendido

This sketch was first performed in 1987, and was reprised in a slightly shortened and simplified form in 1991; it is that later version which is given here. We have found over the years that sketches set at a counter or a desk can provide good opportunites for humorous confrontations: other examples in this book are Sketch 7 *The passport office*, Sketch 9 *The post office*, Sketch 12 *The check-in desk*, and Sketch 16 *A ticket to Birmingham*. In Book 2 examples are Sketch 5 *Tourist information*, and Sketch 9 *The lost property office*.

Words and expressions

Connected with hotels:
reception desk, manager, single room, double room

Other expressions:
insult (vb.), *complain*, *report* (vb.), *I don't like your attitude, unhelpful, unpleasant, horrible, ridiculous*

The sketch includes puns on the words *book* (as a noun, and as a verb in the expression *book a room*), and *free* (meaning both 'unoccupied' and 'gratis').

Preliminary practice

Write on small pieces of paper some two-line exchanges which could take place in a hotel between a guest and a receptionist. For example:
I'd like a single room. – Sorry, we only have double rooms.
Can I have breakfast in my room? – Certainly. What time?
I need to send a fax. – Sorry, the fax machine is out of order.
Is there a swimming-pool in the hotel? – No, but there's a sauna.
I'd like a room with a view of the sea. – Sorry, that's not possible: the sea is 100 miles away.

Distribute the papers to pairs of students. In their pairs, the students work out how to *mime* their exchanges, using just gestures and no words. Then the pairs mime their exchanges for the rest of the class, who try to guess the words.

Follow-up activities

Here is an activity which can be done in groups (of four students, for example). In each group, one student is a hotel receptionist, and the other three are people wishing to book rooms. The receptionist is provided with a cue-card giving information about the hotel, like this, for example:

Single rooms: £25 per night
Double rooms: £40 per night
All rooms have bath or shower. Breakfast included.
Pets not accepted. Car park available.
Restaurant open: 12.00–15.00, 18.00–23.30.
Tonight the hotel is fully booked, but rooms are available for any other night.

Here are some possible texts for the guests' cue-cards:

You want a double room with a shower for next Wednesday night. Ask about the price. Ask if you can bring your two dogs.
You want a single room for tonight and tomorrow night. You will arrive by car, so ask if there is a car park.
You want two single rooms for next Friday and Saturday. You will arrive quite late on the Friday and would like a meal when you arrive.

The guests 'telephone' the receptionist and try to book their rooms. Then a different person in each group is appointed as the receptionist; these new receptionists go to different groups and the activity is repeated.

Props and costumes

For classroom re-enacting, all that is needed is a table (the reception desk), and a large book (the guest registration book which the receptionist consults).

For a performance, the table used for the reception desk could have a large sign on the front reading 'Welcome to the Hotel Splendido: Reception'; the tourist could have a suitcase; and the large guest registration book will also be needed, of course. Costumes: the tourist has shorts and a bright, multi-coloured shirt; the receptionist should be dressed smartly as appropriate to the job.

Hotel Splendido

Scene	The reception desk at a hotel in England
Characters	The receptionist
	An English tourist

The tourist arrives at the reception desk; he is wearing shorts and a very bright, multi-coloured shirt.

Receptionist   Good afternoon, sir. Welcome to the Hotel Splendido.

Tourist   Thank you.

Receptionist   (**Pointing at the tourist**) Good heavens! Look at that!

Tourist   (**Alarmed**) What? Look at what?

The receptionist indicates the tourist's shirt.

Receptionist   Your shirt!

Tourist   My shirt?

Receptionist   Yes!

Tourist   Do you like it?

Receptionist   No!

Tourist   No?

Receptionist   No. It's horrible.

Tourist   I beg your pardon?

Receptionist   It's horrible! But for you, it's a good shirt.

Tourist   Thank you.

Receptionist   Because when people look at you, they look at the shirt.

Tourist   I know.

Receptionist   And that's good – because if they look at the shirt, they don't look at the shorts.

Tourist   What?

Receptionist   And the shorts are *really* horrible.

Tourist   Now, listen. I didn't come here to be insulted by you.

Receptionist   Oh, you want somebody else to do it. (**Calling**) Hey, George, come here for a minute!

Tourist   Stop! Look, I want to book a room.

Receptionist   Book a room?

Tourist   Yes. Have you got one?

Receptionist   What? A book or a room?

Tourist	A room! Have you got a room?
Receptionist	Yes, we've got lots of rooms. It's a big hotel.
Tourist	Yes, but have you got a room *free*?
Receptionist	Free?
Tourist	Yes.
Receptionist	No! You have to pay for it!
Tourist	I mean: Have you got a room with no one in it?
Receptionist	I don't know.
Tourist	Well, can you have a look in the book?
Receptionist	Pardon?
Tourist	Have a look in the book.
Receptionist	A look in the book?
Tourist	Yes. Have a look in the book.
Receptionist	OK.

The receptionist picks up the guest registration book, opens it, looks quickly at it and closes it again.

Receptionist	OK. I've had a look in the book.
Tourist	And what do you think?
Receptionist	It's a nice book.
Tourist	Look! Have you got a room, or haven't you?
Receptionist	OK, OK, OK!

The receptionist looks at the book again.

Receptionist	Yes, we've got a room.
Tourist	Good.
Receptionist	A *single* room.
Tourist	No good. I need a double room.
Receptionist	Ah yes, for you and your shirt.
Tourist	No! For me and my wife. She's arriving this evening.
Receptionist	Ah. (**Looking at the book again**) Yes, we've got a double room.
Tourist	Good! How much is it?
Receptionist	How much?
Tourist	Yes.
Receptionist	(**Demonstrating with her arms**) It's about this long and about this wide and about this high.
Tourist	No! Not how *big*, how *much*?
Receptionist	Ah! Ten pounds.
Tourist	Ten pounds.

Receptionist   Yes. Ten pounds for you, ten pounds for your wife, and fifty pounds for the horrible shirt.

Tourist   Fifty pounds for the shirt?! That's ridiculous!

Receptionist   It's a ridiculous shirt!

Tourist   Now you listen to me. I don't like your attitude.

Receptionist   I don't like your shirt.

Tourist   I'm going to complain to the manager.

Receptionist   She's not here.

Tourist   Where is she?

Receptionist   In hospital.

Tourist   In hospital? Oh dear. Did she have an accident?

Receptionist   Not exactly. She had dinner in the hotel.

Tourist   Well, I would just like to say that you are the most unhelpful, the most unpleasant, the *worst* receptionist that I have met in my life.

Receptionist   (**Pleased**) Thank you very much.

Tourist   And I am going to report you to the manager!

Receptionist   Fine. Shall I give you the phone number of the hospital?

Tourist   Right, that's enough! My wife and I are *not* going to stay at this hotel. I'll go and book a room at the hotel next door.

Receptionist   OK. See you there.

Tourist   Pardon?

Receptionist   I'll see you there.

Tourist   What?

Receptionist   This is my last day at *this* hotel. I lost my job this morning. I start work tomorrow at the hotel next door.

Tourist   (**Leaving**) Oh, no!

Receptionist   See you tomorrow!

© Doug Case, Ken Wilson 1995. Published by Heinemann English Language Teaching. This sheet may be photocopied and used within the class.

The bus stop 15

This sketch, which has been shortened somewhat for the version in this book, was first performed in 1979. The British habit of forming queues at bus stops is often commented on by visitors to Britain, so we decided to write a sketch set in this situation. We also thought that there were amusing possibilities in the use of a phrasebook to make oneself understood, and thus incorporated this idea into the general misunderstandings at the bus stop. (This phrasebook, *English for All Situations*, re-appears in another sketch in Book 2: Sketch 1, *Gerry Thatcher's party*.)

Words and expressions

rob, robber, robbery, thief, gun, pleased, real, pain, back (n.), *teeth, railway station, police station*

Note the uses of the definite and indefinite articles in referring to the bus service (*the 44, the Number 44 bus*) and to a particular bus on the route in question (*a 44, a Number 46*). Note also the sarcastic tone of *You call yourself a robber!*, and the pacifying tone of *All right, all right, all right!*

Preliminary practice

Put the class into several queues. Give the person at the back of each queue a question on a piece of paper (a different question for each queue). The questions should be long, but easily answerable from personal experience, e.g. *When was the last time you spoke to your very first English teacher?* The person at the back of each queue asks the question* to the person in front of them, who then asks the person in front of them, until the question reaches the person at the head of the queue. This person then *answers* the question*, and the answer is passed along the queue until it reaches the back. The person at the back then announces the original question and the answer received: sometimes there will be little connection between them!

*Note: The Q (and A) should be said quietly *over the shoulder*, and each person should say the Q (and A) *once only*.

Follow-up activities

① In the sketch, the student makes a mistake with the words *money* and *Monday*. Here is a follow-up activity based on similar mistakes. Put the students into eight groups and give each group one of the following sets of words written on a piece of paper:

August, September, October, November, Remember.
spring, summer, autumn, window.
one, two, tree, four, five, six, seven, eight.
January, February, Mars, April, May, June.
shirt, socks, shoes, tea, jacket.
bedroom, living-room, bathroom, chicken, dining-room.
green, yellow, red, grey, wait, black, blue.
trousers, hate, dress, coat, scarf.

In their groups, the students decide which word in their list is a mistake (i.e. *Remember* should be *December*, *window* should be *winter*, etc.). They then invent a sentence including that mistake, e.g. *Christmas Day is Remember 25th, Skiing is a popular window sport*, etc. Each group then reads their sentence to the rest of the class, who have to identify the mistake by saying 'Not *Remember – December*' or '*Window* should be *winter*', etc.

② The students may also like to improvise a sketch in which a robber goes into a bank and uses a phrasebook – either an English robber attempting to rob a bank in their country, or a robber of their nationality attempting to rob a bank in Britain.

Props and costumes

For classroom re-enacting, these props are useful: a small piece of paper or card (the robber's 'business card'); a toy gun (or something to represent it); a book (representing the phrasebook), in which the 'Dialogue I' text could be pasted.

For a performance, you will need: the business card, the gun, the phrasebook (with the title *English for All Situations* on the cover), a whistle for the policeman, a bus stop (this could be a wooden or cardboard sign fixed to a support such as a lampstand). Costumes: in addition to a uniform for the policeman, these could include a college or university T-shirt for the student, a striped sweater for the robber, and a handbag for the old lady. The sound of the buses passing can be made by the old lady and the robber.

The bus stop

Scene	A bus stop
Characters	An old lady
	A robber
	A student
	A policeman

The robber is waiting at the bus stop. The old lady joins him.

Old lady	Excuse me.
Robber	Yes?
Old lady	The 44.
Robber	The 44?
Old lady	Yes. The Number 44 bus. Does it stop here?
Robber	I don't know.

He looks at the notice on the bus stop.

Robber	Um…39…40…41…42…43…45. No, it doesn't.
Old lady	Pardon?
Robber	The 44 doesn't stop here.
Old lady	Oh, good.
Robber	Pardon?
Old lady	I said 'Oh, good'. I'm very pleased.
Robber	What do you mean?
Old lady	I don't want to catch a 44.

She laughs. The robber is not pleased, and stands with his back to her.

Old lady	Excuse me again.
Robber	Yes?
Old lady	The 46.
Robber	The 46?
Old lady	Yes. The Number 46 bus. Does it stop here?
Robber	Do you want to catch a 46?
Old lady	Um…Yes.

The robber looks at the notice again.

Robber	42, 43, 45…45A, 45B, 45C, 45D…46. Yes. Yes, the 46 stops here.

Old lady	Oh, good.
Robber	Ah, here comes a 46 now.

A bus passes very fast.

Old lady	It didn't stop!
Robber	I know.
Old lady	But you said the 46 stopped here. You're telling lies!
Robber	No, I'm not. That one was full. Ah, here comes another one.
Old lady	A Number 1? I don't want a Number 1. I want a Number 46.
Robber	I didn't say 'A Number 1'. I said 'Another one'. Another Number 46.
Old lady	Oh, I see.
Robber	This one will stop.

Another bus passes very fast.

Old lady	It didn't stop!
Robber	I know.

The robber stands with his back to the old lady.

Old lady	Excuse me again.
Robber	No!
Old lady	Pardon?
Robber	No! The 47 doesn't stop here –
Old lady	No, no, no.
Robber	– or the 48, or the 49, or the 50!
Old lady	No, you don't understand. I want to ask you a question.
Robber	Oh, yes?
Old lady	Are you a doctor?
Robber	What?
Old lady	Are you a doctor?
Robber	No, I'm not.
Old lady	Are you sure you're not a doctor?
Robber	Yes, I am!
Old lady	Oh, you *are* a doctor!
Robber	No! I'm *sure* I am *not* a doctor!
Old lady	Oh. What a shame. You see, I've got this terrible pain in my back.
Robber	Well, I'm sorry. I am not a doctor. I am a robber.
Old lady	A what?
Robber	A robber – a thief.

Old lady	Teeth? No, no, not my *teeth* – my *back*. The pain's in my back. My teeth are all right.
Robber	No! I didn't say 'teeth'. I said 'thief'. Thief – robber! I am a robber. Look – here's my card.

He gives her his card.

Old lady	(***Reading***) 'Sam Poskins. Robber. Banks a speciality.' Oh, you're a robber.
Robber	That's right.

He takes back his card.

Old lady	Help!
Robber	What's the matter?
Old lady	Police!!
Robber	Stop it!
Old lady	Murder!!!
Robber	Look – be quiet. It's all right. I rob banks. I don't rob people. And I certainly don't rob old ladies.
Old lady	Old ladies!
Robber	Yes.
Old lady	Old ladies! *I'm* not an old lady. I'm only 92.
Robber	Well, I don't care if you're 92 or 192. I am *not* going to rob you.
Old lady	I don't believe you.
Robber	What?
Old lady	I don't believe you're a robber.
Robber	Well, I *am*.
Old lady	No, no, no – impossible.
Robber	What do you mean?
Old lady	You're too small.
Robber	What do you mean – I'm 'too small'? I am *not* too small.
Old lady	Yes, you are. You're *much* too small.
Robber	No, I'm not. And anyway, I've got a gun. Look!

He takes out his gun.

Old lady	Oh, yes. You've got a gun.
Robber	That's right.
Old lady	Help!
Robber	It's all right. It's not real.
Old lady	Not real?!
Robber	No.
Old lady	You call yourself a robber! You're too small, your gun isn't real, and you can't even rob a 92-year-old lady at a bus stop!

Robber	All right, all right, all right! I'll *show* you. I will rob the next person who comes to this bus stop.
Old lady	Oh, good!...Look – here comes someone.
Robber	Right. Watch this.

The student stands at the bus stop, holding a book.

Robber	Excuse me.
Student	Yes?
Robber	Put up your hands.
Student	I'm sorry. I don't speak English.
Robber	Oh. Er...Give me your money.
Student	What?
Robber	Your money!
Student	Money?
Robber	Yes – money, money, money!
Student	Ah! No, it's not *Money*...it's *Tuesday*.
Robber	No, no, no. I didn't say 'Monday'. I said 'money'. Money!
Student	No. I told you – it isn't Money, it's Tuesday. Look – it's in this book.

The student opens the book.

| **Student** | Money, Tuesday... |

The robber takes the book.

| **Robber** | What is this book? 'English for all situations'. Oh, good. |

He looks through the book.

| **Robber** | Um...'In a restaurant'...'On a train'...Ah, yes – this is it: 'Unit 16. The robbery.' Good. Look – here. 'Dialogue 1: Give me your money.' |

The student reads in the book too.

Student	Ah, *money*! Um...'Are you trying to rob me?'
Robber	'Yes, I am.'
Student	'Are you a robber?'
Robber	'Yes, I am.'
Student	'I will call a policeman.'
Robber	'No, you won't.'
Student	'Yes, I will.'
Robber	'No, you won't.'...'Policemen are like buses. You can never find one when you want one.'
Student	'No, you are wrong. There's a policeman standing behind you.'

This is true.

Robber	Ha, ha! I don't believe *that*!…Oh.
Policeman	Now, what's going on here?
Robber	Ah. Er…well…

The robber, the student and the old lady all talk at once. The policeman blows his whistle.

Policeman	Right. You can all come with me to the station.
Robber	Oh, no!
Student	Oh, yes – 'Unit 17: The police station.'
Old lady	Station? I don't want to catch a train. I want to catch a Number 46 bus.
Policeman	Not the *railway* station, madam – the *police* station.
Old lady	Oh, the police station! Yes, I know it. It's very near my house. Come on, everybody!

The robber, the student and the old lady walk away, all talking at once again. The policeman follows them, blowing his whistle.

© Doug Case, Ken Wilson 1995. Published by Heinemann English Language Teaching. This sheet may be photocopied and used within the class.

Having noticed that people in several countries tend to make jokes about railway services in the way that has become traditional in Britain about British Rail, we wrote this sketch. It was first performed in 1979, and the version in this book is substantially the same as the stage version. As is clear from several sketches in this collection, we are quite fond of situations in which one character seeks to prevent another from achieving some theoretically easy objective (see also Sketch 12 *The check-in desk* and Sketch 14 *Hotel Splendido*, for example).

Words and expressions

lovely, terrible, awful, ridiculous, second-class, single, ticket office, platform, miss (a train)
plenty of time, in a hurry, There's no hurry

The sketch includes several conditional sentences (e.g. *You'll get very tired if you run*), including the type used for giving advice beginning: *If I were you, I'd... .*

Note the use of present tenses for 'fixed timetables' or 'future arrangements': *What time does the train leave?, The train's leaving any minute now.*

Preliminary practice

In the sketch, the railway employee seems to wilfully avoid doing the simple thing, i.e. selling the traveller a ticket. It may be enjoyable for the class to engage in some similar wilful avoidance.

Tell the students that they are going to ask each other for something – it can be an object they wish to borrow, a favour, a piece of information, etc. – and that the students who are addressed must think of ways of *not* lending the object, *not* granting the favour, *not* giving the information, etc. For example, if Student **A** asks: *What time is it?*, Student **B** could reply: *Why do you want to know?* or *Doesn't time go quickly when you're having fun?* or *You know, I must buy a new watch.* Give each student the chance to ask a question and also to avoid answering one.

Follow-up activities

① The students may like to improvise a sketch of their own, in which someone wants to buy a ticket of another kind – a rock concert ticket, for example – and the ticket-seller attempts to dissuade them.

② In pairs or in groups, the students could complete the brief telephone conversations from the sketch, in which only the British Rail employee's words are given. There are six such conversations, and all are introduced in the script by the phrase *On the phone.* (The pairs or groups could take one or two different conversations each, or all the pairs/groups could have the same conversation(s).)

The students should write out the BR employee's words as given in the script, leaving a line for each reply (represented by three dots in the script), and then decide what the other speaker said. When they have completed their conversations, the pairs or groups could read them out to the rest of the class.

③ In pairs, the students could of course simply improvise some conversations in which they buy a railway ticket in the normal way, i.e. without any of the problems which arise in the sketch because of the BR employee's delaying tactics. The conversation would cover the destination, the type of ticket required (first- or second-class, single or return), the price, how the traveller wants to pay, etc.

Props and costumes

For simple classroom re-enacting, the only props required are a table, two chairs, a newspaper for the employee at the beginning (although this is not vital), and a telephone.

For a more elaborate performance, the above props will be needed, plus costumes for the characters: the employee should have a railway uniform jacket, and possibly a cap; the traveller's costume can be as desired. The traveller could also have a suitcase or a rucksack. Note that the telephone has to ring during the sketch.

A ticket to Birmingham

Scene   A railway station in Britain
Characters   A traveller
                    A British Rail employee

The BR employee is sitting at a table, reading a newspaper. The traveller comes in.

Traveller	Excuse me.
BR employee	Can I help you?
Traveller	Yes. I want a ticket.
BR employee	A ticket?
Traveller	Yes. I want a ticket to Birmingham.
BR employee	A ticket to Birmingham?
Traveller	Yes.
BR employee	Why?
Traveller	Why what?
BR employee	Why do you want a ticket to Birmingham?
Traveller	Well –
BR employee	Birmingham's a terrible place! It's awful! If I were you, I wouldn't go to Birmingham.
Traveller	I live there.
BR employee	Now, Oxford's a very nice place.
Traveller	I *live* there.
BR employee	Why don't you go to Oxford?
Traveller	I *live* there!
BR employee	What? In Oxford?
Traveller	No! In Birmingham!
BR employee	Oh.
Traveller	And I want to go to Birmingham. Today.
BR employee	Impossible.
Traveller	What?
BR employee	It's impossible. It'll take you three days.
Traveller	Three days?
BR employee	Oh, yes. It'll take you at least three days – walking.
Traveller	Walking?! I don't want to *walk* to Birmingham!
BR employee	You don't want to walk?

Traveller	No.
BR employee	Oh, I understand.
Traveller	Good.
BR employee	You want to run.
Traveller	Run?!
BR employee	You'll get very tired if you run.
Traveller	Listen –
BR employee	If I were you, I'd walk.
Traveller	I don't want to walk, and I don't want to run. I want to take the train.
BR employee	The train? Ha! You'll get there much faster if you walk.
Traveller	Now, don't be ridiculous. I want a ticket for the next train to Birmingham.
BR employee	The next train to Birmingham?
Traveller	Yes. When is it?
BR employee	Pardon?
Traveller	What time is it?
BR employee	I don't know. I haven't got a watch.
Traveller	No! I mean: What time is the train? What time does the train leave?
BR employee	Oh, I see. Sorry. I'll check.

He picks up the telephone and dials a number.

BR employee	Take a seat.
Traveller	Thank you.

The traveller sits down.

BR employee	(**On the phone**) Hello? Bert?…Who's that?…Oh, hello, Charlie. Where's Bert?…Is he? Oh, well, is Eric there?…Hello? Eric?…Isn't Bert there?…Oh, dear – very sad. Is Arthur there?…Hello? Arthur?…Who? Oh, hello, Charlie. Is Bert there?

The traveller is getting impatient.

Traveller	Look – can you please find out when the next train to Birmingham leaves?
BR employee	Yes, all right. (**On the phone**) Er…Charlie…Who's that? Eric?…Oh, Arthur. Can I speak to Dave?…Yes, OK, I'll hold on.

The traveller is getting more impatient.

Traveller	Look –
BR employee	It's all right. I'm holding on. (**On the phone**) Dave?…Hello, Dave. This is Sid…Very well, thanks – and you?…Good. Listen, Dave, there's something I must ask you. How's your wife?…Did she?
Traveller	The next train to Birmingham!
BR employee	Oh, yes. (**On the phone**) Dave, I've got a young man here. When is the next train to Birmingham? Yes…Yes…Yes…Yes…Yes. Thanks, Dave. Hold on.

Traveller	Well?
BR employee	He doesn't know.
Traveller	He doesn't know?
BR employee	No.
Traveller	Why not?
BR employee	Well, Dave doesn't work at the station.
Traveller	He doesn't work at the station?!
BR employee	No. Dave works at the café across the road. You should never ask Dave about trains.
Traveller	*I* didn't ask him. *You* asked him!
BR employee	*Eric's* the one who knows about trains.
Traveller	Well, ask *Eric* then.
BR employee	Right. (**On the phone**) Er...Dave, can you put Eric back on?...Eric?...Eric, I've got a young man here. It's about trains to Birmingham. When is the next one? ...Right...OK...Fine...Super...Smashing...Super...Fine...OK...Right. Thanks, Eric. Bye.

He puts down the telephone.

Traveller	So, when is the train?
BR employee	The train, yes. Well, there's a small problem.
Traveller	What's that?
BR employee	They can't find it.
Traveller	They can't find what?
BR employee	They can't find the train. It's lost.
Traveller	Lost?!
BR employee	Well, it's not exactly *lost*. They know where it is.
Traveller	Well, where is it?
BR employee	It's somewhere between here and Birmingham.
Traveller	This is terrible.
BR employee	Yes, but it happens every day. If I were you, I'd start walking.
Traveller	But I'm in a hurry.
BR employee	Well, run then.
Traveller	I don't want to run.
BR employee	Well, take a taxi!
Traveller	I don't want to take a taxi!

The telephone rings. The traveller answers it.

Traveller	Hello!!!...It's for you.

The BR employee takes the telephone.

BR employee   Thank you. (**On the phone**) Hello? Sid speaking. Who's that?…Eric! Hello! What is it?…The train to Birmingham?…What?…Marvellous. Where was it?…At Platform 2?…It was there all the time. Amazing…OK, Eric, I'll tell him. Bye.

He puts down the telephone.

BR employee   Well, there *is* a train to Birmingham.

Traveller   Marvellous.

BR employee   It's at Platform 2.

Traveller   Wonderful.

BR employee   And it's leaving any minute now.

Traveller   Oh, good. A second-class single to Birmingham, please.

BR employee   Pardon?

Traveller   Can you give me a second-class single to Birmingham?

BR employee   No, I can't.

Traveller   Why not?

BR employee   Well, this isn't the ticket office.

Traveller   What?!

BR employee   The ticket office is next door.

Traveller   Oh, no!

BR employee   What's the matter?

Traveller   I'm going to miss the train!

BR employee   Don't worry. You've got plenty of time.

Traveller   Plenty of time? The train's leaving any minute now.

BR employee   Yes, but there's no hurry.

Traveller   Why not?

BR employee   Because I'm the driver.

Traveller   You're the driver?!

BR employee   Yes. The train can't leave without me, can it?

Traveller   No.

BR employee   Now, you come with me.

Traveller   Platform 2?

BR employee   No. Dave's café.

Traveller   Oh, right.

BR employee   We'll have a nice cup of tea and a sandwich before we go.

Traveller   Lovely.

BR employee   And I'll introduce you to Dave and his wife. I think you'll like them…

They leave, chatting.

Notes and reminders

Notes and reminders

Heinemann Questionnaire

At Heinemann ELT we are committed to continuing research into materials development. We would be very interested to hear your feedback about this resource book. Please photocopy this form and send it to your local Heinemann office or to the address at the bottom of the form. Thank you for your help.

Name:	**Course materials currently used with class**
Name of school:	....
Address of school:	....
Average age of students:	**Supplementary materials currently used with class:**
Size of class:	....
Frequency and length of lesson:	....

Please tell us if you have enjoyed using this photocopiable teacher's resource book. If not, please tell us why not; if you have, please tell us why.

....

....

....

What features do you like most about this resource book? What do you like least?

....

....

....

Do you have any suggestions for improvements?

....

....

....

What other kinds of materials would you like to see in a photocopiable format?

....

....

....

Please check the boxes below if you would like information about new materials or would like to help us in materials development.

I would like to receive information about new materials for ...	**Would you be willing to help us develop new materials to suit your needs? Yes, I would like to ...**
☐ children ☐ adults	☐ **pilot materials in my classroom.**
☐ exams ☐ readers	☐ **answer questionnaires.**
☐ **secondary school students**	☐ **discuss my needs with a Heinemann Representative.**
☐ **university students**	
☐ **business English**	
☐ **supplementary materials**	

Please return this form to:
Editor, Heinemann Teacher Resources, Heinemann ELT, Halley Court, Jordan Hill, Oxford OX2 8EJ, UK
If you would prefer to fax the form, please send to + 44 1865 314193.

EAR TRAINING

ONE NOTE

COMPLETE METHOD

by
Bruce Arnold

Muse Eek Publishing Company
New York, New York

ISBN 1-890944-47-5

Printed in the United States

This publication can be purchased from your local bookstore or by contacting:
Muse Eek Publishing Company
P.O. Box 509
New York, NY 10276, USA
Phone: 212-473-7030
Fax: 212-473-4601
http://www.muse-eek.com
sales@muse-eek.com

Table Of Contents

Acknowledgments

The author would like to thank Michal Shapiro for proof reading and helpful suggestions. I would also like to thank my students who through their questions helped me to see their needs so that I might address them as best I could.

About the Author

Bruce Arnold is from Sioux Falls, South Dakota. His educational background started with 3 years of music study at the University of South Dakota; he then attended the Berklee College of Music where he received a Bachelor of Music degree in composition. During that time he also studied privately with Jerry Bergonzi and Charlie Banacos.

Mr. Arnold has taught at some of the most prestigious music schools in America, including the New England Conservatory of Music, Dartmouth College, Berklee College of Music, Princeton University and New York University. He is a performer, composer, jazz clinician and has an extensive private instruction practice.

Currently Mr. Arnold is performing with his own "The Bruce Arnold Trio," and "Eye Contact" with Harvie Swartz, as well as with two experimental bands, "Release the Hounds" a free improv group, and "Spooky Actions" which re-interprets the work of 20th Century classical masters.

His debut CD "Blue Eleven" (MMC 2036J) received great critical acclaim, and his most recent CD "A Few Dozen" was released in January 2000. The Los Angeles Times said of this release "Mr. Arnold deserves credit for his effort to expand the jazz palette."

For more information about Mr. Arnold check his website at http://www.arnoldjazz.com This website contains audio examples of Mr. Arnold's compositions and a workshop section with free downloadable music exercises.

Foreword

This ear training series presents a method that I have found to successfully change a student's ability to identify pitches. There is a direct correlation between this ability and their musicality. This method will help you on your way to achieving master musicianship. This book contains all the the information found in the following three books "One Note Ear Training Beginning, Intermediate and Advanced." It is geared towards the beginning student who is expected to progress through all 3 CDs contained herein. Each CD has the same type of exercises but the speed at which each exercise plays doubles

In order to use this type of ear training with real music you need to develop your aural skills so that you can quickly identify notes in relationship to their key center. When you reach the Advanced level CD and feel you are getting around 80% correct it is time to move on to the book "Key Note Recognition" which will help prepare you for the "Ear Training Two Note Series."

It is important that you first read pages 1-13 before you attempt to listen to the CD. The information presented on these pages is integral to understanding the right way to approach this ear training method.

You will also find the FAQs (Frequently Asked Questions) starting on page 17 to be a good source for answering any questions you might have about this method. Muse Eek Publishing Company hosts two on-line resources in conjunction with this book. A "Frequently Asked Questions" page (FAQ) is available where students can ask questions that may arise as they work. There is also a free "member's section" where book owners can download other files specific to this book and/or other help files to further their music education.

Bruce Arnold
New York, New York

Before We Start

Whether you are working with the "Ear Training One Note Series" or the "Fanatic's Guide to Ear Training and Sight Singing" you must have a certain amount of basic musical knowledge in order to use this ear training method efficiently.

If you are a music student who already knows the names of all 12 notes and how they relate to a key, what the diatonic chords of a key are and how they can be used to form a cadence in a key, which in turns establishes a key in your mind, you may skip this section and go on to page 9.

If you are a total beginner to music it is important to understand that in order to develop your ear and your musical abilities to a high level you will need to have at least a basic understanding of music theory. **If you don't understand the rudiments of how music is put together you won't understand or be able to work with this ear training method.** For instance, each track of the "One Note Ear Training" CD plays a group of chords, and then plays a note. The group of chords are there to establish a "sense of key" in your mind. Why are we using this particular group of chords to establish a "key" and what is a "sense of key" anyway? Well, you have to understand some basic music theory before that will make any sense to you. After you hear this group of chords you hear a note and then you need to guess what that note is. If you don't know the names of all possible notes then you won't know what answer to give. Let's say you <u>do</u> know the names of the 12 pitches we use in western music but you don't know what relationship they have to a "key" or you are a little fuzzy on what exactly a "key" or "sense of key" is. These problems can only be solved effectively by learning some music theory.

<u>Don't Panic!</u> The good news is you don't need a year long course in music theory to understand this ear training; you just need a certain amount of information so you can use this ear training in a beneficial way. Of course the more you understand all the ins and outs of music theory the more you will realize different ways of applying the notes you hear, so I highly recommend you take your music theory past the level presented here. On page eight I make some suggestions for books that will help you understand music theory on a deeper level. If you study from these books you will raise your level of musicianship up so the ear training you learn here can be even more useful.

The main thing you must learn from a cursory knowledge of music theory is what the notes are, how pitches are organized, how they relate to a "key," what a 'key' is and how a "sense of key" is established. When you get this organized in your head you will be at a point where the ear training can be applied to music.

If you still don't quite understand why you need this basic music theory knowledge let me give you an analogy. Imagine you go to a country where they speak a language you don't know, and just learn to say a bunch of short sentences that a friend taught you. You know the basic meaning of each phrase, like "I'd like some coffee" or "may I have the check?" But you don't know what each word is or how these words are combined. You just know the sound and what it means. This might help you as you sit in a restaurant and the waitress walks up to take your order. BUT, what if she asks you which type of coffee you want and whether you want cream and sugar. Not only won't you understand what she is saying you won't know how to answer her. It is the same way with learning the sound of all 12 notes. You could just memorize the sound of each note but then what? The reason you are learning these sounds is so you can apply them. This application comes in many forms: are you able to find these notes on your instrument, are you able to use this ear training knowledge to interact with other musicians? Do you understand how to write these notes down on paper if you are creating a composition? You can see from these situations that you really need to know more than just what a note is.

1

Let me give you another example of why knowing music theory is important in a real life musical situation. Let's say you have a band member who just played you a couple of notes and tells you to use these notes as a guide and create a solo or melody around these notes. He also mentions that you can add in some others notes if you would like. So let's say with your ear training ability you realize what notes he is playing and you also figured out that he is in the key of C major and let's say that the notes were G, E, F, D and B. So obviously you can combine these 5 notes in different ways as a first step towards complying with your band member's request. But what are the other available notes that would sound good? What do you do if he asks you to also play a chord that goes with these notes if you are a piano or guitar player? What do you do then? Well, you will have a problem if you don't know some music theory and realize that the D, E, F, G and B could only be from a C major scale and that therefore if you wanted to add in a couple of new notes you could add a C and an A. If you want to play a chord over these notes you would need to know that these notes are from the C major scale. With that knowledge you could play a C chord or another chord derived from the scale. You can see how by knowing music theory you can expand your ear training a lot. **Understanding music theory will allow you to recognize the context from which the notes you are hearing come, or can be put into.** Therefore you can see that music theory will greatly expand your application of the notes you hear.

Getting back to the basics again; if you hear a few notes, and can identify these from working with ear training, do you then know where these notes are on your instrument? This presents yet another task; you need to learn where all 12 notes are on your instrument. You need to know this in at least the key of C major to work with the "Ear Training One Note Series" and also how they relate to all twelve keys if you are working with the advanced parts of the "Fanatic's Guide to Ear Training and Sight Singing" Book.

To Recap: I think from all these examples you can see that to fully develop your ear you need to have at least a basic understanding of music theory. This rudimentary understanding means that you know how all 12 notes relate to each other, you have a grasp on such basic concepts as "key" and the knowledge of how each note relates to a "key center." In order to get started with this process we need to get you to understand music from the ground up.

I strongly recommend you also use an instrument on which to work with all this music theory information. Though not a requirement, if you have access to a keyboard of some sort, this will be extremely helpful, since the diagrams used to demonstrate the musical concepts are based on a piano keyboard. You will also find a free educational file call "Applying Music Theory" in the member's section of the Muse-eek.com website that will give you many exercises to help you apply music theory to your instrument. Remember this process of learning music theory will take some effort on your part. Have patience, and you will get a working knowledge of the basic mechanics. Take the information in slowly, try applying it to your instrument till you "hear" each theoretical concept. With this in mind let's get started with learning the basics of music theory!

Music Theory and Ear Training

We first need to understand how music is written down in order to present the basic concepts of music theory. Try to memorize each example so you don't have to constantly relate back to it. This will take a little time and effort on your part but will be very rewarding in the long run.

Example 1 shows a series of lines and spaces which are employed to create a visual representation of sound. Each line and space corresponds to a pitch. Each pitch is given a name A, B, C, D, E, F, or G. (There is no H, I, J, K etc.). A clef sign is also used to designate what names each line and space will receive. There are many types of clefs but we will only concern ourselves with the treble clef. This complete system of lines and spaces with a clef sign is called a "staff".

Example 1

As can be seen in Example 1, each line and space corresponds to a different tone. If you want to have pitches higher or lower than the 5 lines and four spaces shown in example one, you can extend the staff by using ledger lines. Ledger lines give you the ability to represent higher and lower pitches by extending the staff; these extended pitches are called ledger line notes. (See Example 2)

Example 2

It is not that important right now to learn how to read ledger lines but it is important to realize that all 12 notes repeat themselves in different "octaves."

What is an octave? If we look at our treble clef again (Example 1) we notice that there is an "e" on the first line and a "e" on the 4th space. Our ear recognizes these pitches as being the same pitch but the "e" on the 4th space sounds like a higher version of the low "e". In musical terminology the higher "e" is said to sound an octave higher than the lower "e". Example 3 show where these two "e's" would be located on a piano keyboard.

Example 3

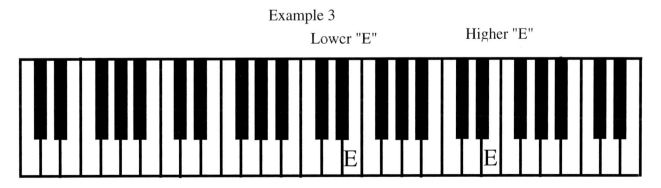

If you don't understand how notes are laid out on the piano keyboard see page 5.

To summarize what we have learned so far: there are 7 pitches which are represented on a staff with the letter names A,B,C,D,E,F,G. These 7 pitches keep repeating themselves in different octaves. As you start to work with the "One Note Ear Training" CD you will notice that many of the pitches in each exercise are in different octaves. For example, track one and track seventeen on the CD are both D's but are found in different octaves. Another way to understand an octave is that if you count from E to E on the keyboard, the sum is 8 and an octave equals 8 (see example 8 on page 6 to help you visualize this).

One of the inconsistencies of the notation system we have learned so far is that it doesn't show all the available notes in western music. There are a total of 12 pitches used in western music which of course as we have learned can be found in many different octaves. To show all 12 notes in the system, "sharp"(#) and "flat" (b) symbols are used to represent the tones that occur between the letter names of the notes. For example between the note C and D there exists a pitch which can be called either C sharp or D flat. These notes are represented as follows: C# or Db. The (#) and (b) symbols work in the following way, the flat (b) lowers a pitch and a sharp (#) which raises the pitch. If a note is sharped it is said to have been raised a half step; if it is flatted it is said to have been lowered a half step. **A half step is the smallest distance possible in western music.** If we show all 12 notes on the staff within one octave we get what is called the chromatic scale. (See example 4) This scale contains all possible notes in the western system of music. Notice that there is no sharp or flat between E and F and B and C which is just one of those inconsistencies you have to accept with this notation system. On our piano keyboard the E and F and B and C occur between the groups of black notes (see example 5 on page 5). Both chromatic scales shown below sound the same on the piano; the decision to use sharps or flats depends on the musical situation. If a note is not flatted or sharped it is called "natural." You will notice in Example 4 that the D in the chromatic scale with flats has a symbol in front of it. This symbol is called a "natural" sign. It is used to cancel the flat that appears before the previous D. **In written music, measures are used to delineate time, and sharps and flats carry through the whole measure until a new measure starts, unless a natural symbol is used to cancel it.**

Example 4   **Chromatic Scale**

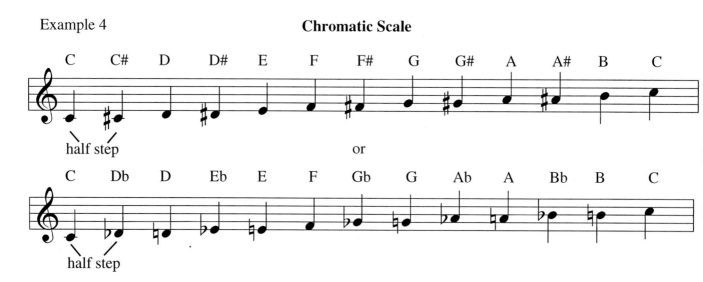

If you are using the "One Note Ear Training Series" play a few tracks and see if you can find the notes for each track in the Chromatic scale shown in Example 4. If you are using the "Fanatic's Guide to Ear Training and Sight Singing" make sure you understand how each note you sing is related to the chromatic scale. Which ever book you are using you need to memorize the names of all the notes found in the chromatic scale so when you hear or sing them you know what they are.

The 12 note chromatic scale can be represented using either method found in Example 4. Remember a C# is the same note as a Db on the piano. If you play a C chromatic scale on the piano you would move consecutively up the piano keyboard starting on C (See Example 5). Remember the distance between each note of the chromatic scale is called a half step and the distance between each note of the piano is also a half step. Notice that sometimes this half step occurs between white and black notes and sometimes between two white notes.

Example 5

Chromatic Scale of the Piano Keyboard.

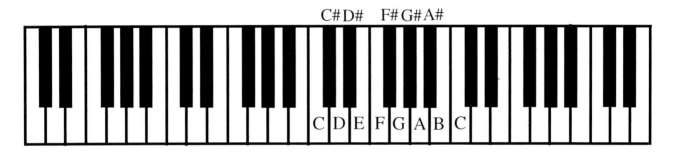

Though the chromatic scale represents all 12 notes, much of western music of the last few centuries has been based around only 7 tones. If we extract these 7 notes as shown in Example 6 we end up with what is called a major scale.

Example 6

Major scale derived from Chromatic scale

Chromatic Scale

Major Scale

If we look at the distance in half steps between the notes of a major scale we see a pattern; whole *, whole, half, whole, whole, whole, half. **All major scales are based on these intervals** (See Example 7).

Example 7   **C Major Scale**

whole step   whole step   half step   whole step   whole step   whole step   half step

* NOTE: Two half steps equals a whole step.

If we apply the major scale to the piano keyboard the system works out as follows: start on any note on the piano and move up a whole step (2 half steps), whole step, half step, whole step, whole step, whole step, half step. Example 8 shows how a C major scale would look on a piano keyboard. If you are not using a piano play a c major scale on your instrument.

Example 8

With this information you could play any major scale by following the pattern of whole step, whole step, half step, whole step, whole step, whole step, half step. The notes of a C major scale C, D, E, F, G, A, B are commonly referred to as the <u>diatonic</u> notes of the key of C major.

The reason it is so important to understand what a major scale is and how it is constructed is that when these notes are combined a certain pattern it creates the sense of a "key" in our musical mind. It takes time to develop this sense or feeling of key but is an important part of understanding the ear training process. We will talk more about this in a moment but first we need to talk about how you can play specific notes of the C major scale at the same time to form chords.

A chord can be a combination of any 3 or more notes played at the same time. These chords can be built in a variety of ways. One of the most common ways to build chords is to stack up alternating notes of the C major scale. For example if we took C from our C major scale and stacked up every other note we would get C, E, and G. Example 9 shows how these would look on the musical staff.

Example 9

C Major Triad *

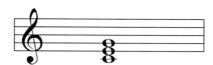

* These 3 note structures are commonly referred to as triads and the C note is said to be the root of the chord.

If we continue this process and build up triads above all the notes of a C major scale we get the following 3 note structures (See Example 10)

Example 10

Triads derived from stacking 3rds above a C major scale

Each of these 3 note structures has a name assigned to it and these chords are known as the **diatonic chords of the key of C major.** Example 11 shows you the names of these chords.

Example 11

The names for each triad in a C major scale

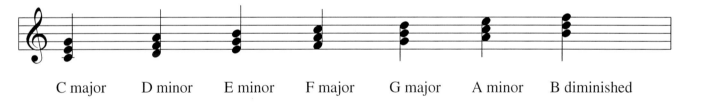

C major   D minor   E minor   F major   G major   A minor   B diminished

For our purposes is not crucial that you understand why each of these chords has its particular name or how they are constructed. What is important is that you realize that when we combine a group of these chords into a particular sequence of chords they create the sense of "key" in our mind. For example if we play a C major chord to an F major chord, then a G major chord back to a C major chord we instantly create the sense of the key of C major in the mind. Although at this point this may not seem obvious to you now, over time you will start to develop this sense of key. When we play this chord combination of C to F to G to C we are playing what is referred to as a **"cadence."** There are many types of chord cadences in music but for now we will just deal with the aforementioned cadence. You will notice on the Ear Training books that each track always starts out with this C to F to G to C cadence. **Hearing this cadence places your mind into the key of C major so when you hear the note that follows you relate this note to the key of C major.** It will take you time to develop this sense of key and to hear how each note relates to it, but this is the process that you are attempting to master whether you are using the "Ear Training One Note Series" CD or the "Fanatic's Guide to Ear Training and Sight Singing" CD.

With this new understanding of "key" we need to go back to our chromatic scale and review what each pitch's name would be in relationship to the key of C. Example 12 shows the C chromatic scale with note names. As you hear the examples on the CD you need to choose which one of these pitches are being played .

Example 12

Chromatic Scale

Each one of these pitches has a signature sound within the "key." It will take time before you "hear" this but be patient with yourself.

Key Versus Interval

Now that you are acquainted with how a major scale is constructed, and how certain notes combined into a cadence places your mind into a key, it is important to talk a moment about how other ear training methods teach you to learn the sound of each note. Many ear training methods tell you to learn the distance between each note rather than the sound of each note within a key. The distance between each note is called an interval. For example, in example 12 the interval between C and C# is called a minor second, the distance between C and D is called a major second etc.. It is not important for the type of ear training used in the "One Note Ear Training Series" or the "Fanatic's Guide to Ear Training and Sight Singing" to know intervals. In both of the aforementioned books the "Teaching Methods" section explains the differences between these two ear training methods. Understanding the "Teaching Methods" section's extensive explanation of why hearing by "key" is a much better system of ear training than using intervals is really important in order to progress with this ear training method. The music theory information you have just learned should help you to understand the difference between these two methods of developing your aural perception.

*   *   *

The explanation of music theory presented here is rudimentary and is only meant to help a total beginner understand how to approach this ear training method. It is recommended that you work with a music theory book in order to gain a more thorough working knowledge of the mechanics of music. I suggest Music Theory Workbook for All Instruments Volume One ISBN #1890944467 or 1890944920 or for guitarists there is the Music Theory Workbook for Guitar Volume One ISBN #0964863219 or 1890944505

Teaching Methods

There are many different approaches to developing pitch. Some of these methods are successful, some are not. First you must decide what kind of ear training will fit your needs. If you are a classical musician playing 20th century pieces that require you to play what may seem like random pitches with very few reference pitches to help you with intonation, you may find that developing perfect pitch is the most important goal for you. If you are a contemporary rock or jazz player playing improvised music you will find that developing relative pitch is far more important because it allows you to identify the keys that vamps, melodies and free improvisations are in, so you can respond with appropriate melodies or chords.

Commonly most courses of study for relative pitch concentrate on music dictation and singing melodies. Most colleges and high schools teach this way. But there are very real pitfalls to this method; most of these courses of study prepare a student to pass an exam but don't prepare a working musician for the skills they will need in a working situation. These courses fail to explain what to be listening for, and instead encourage the use of common tricks. These in turn lead to habits which stunt the student's progress. In some ways it is better if you've never done any ear training before starting the method presented here, because you won't have had a chance to develop the bad habits incorrect instruction can lead to.

Let's us talk about some of these teaching methods and why they simply do not work in the real world.

One of the most counterproductive assignments relative pitch ear training courses assign is to "learn all your intervals."

A teacher sits down at a piano and starts playing different intervals and asks the class to identify which interval is being played. You may ask "What's so bad about that? All music is made up of different combinations of intervals so this should help me to identify pitch, right?"

Let's look closer. Let's say you have mastered this assignment; and any interval someone plays, you know what it is instantly. All right, great! Now you are on the band stand and the piano player is jamming along on a C major chord over and over and the bass player is playing a C note over and over. Most students with a little theory or practical experience know that playing a C chord over and over means the piece is in the key of C. Now your guitar player plays two notes which happen to be an E and a G. You instantly say "that's a minor 3rd that I hear. (The distance between E and G being 3 half steps which is commonly referred to as a minor 3rd) "All right" says the guitar player "well play it then," but now the real question has to be answered: what minor 3rd is it? If we examine the 12 pitches used in western music we find that there are 12 possible minor 3rd intervals that we could choose from. For example C to Eb, C# to E, D to F— all of these are minor 3rd intervals, and there are 12 possible minor 3rd intervals in all.

How do you know which one it is?

The answer is you <u>don't</u> because you have only learned what a minor 3rd sounds like and not what the two pitches E and G sound like in the key. So something is missing here. You need to know more than what an interval sounds like; you need to know what notes sound like <u>in a key</u>. This is the first and major difference between the ear training contained in this book and that which is commonly taught in schools.

So, back to our example: if you knew what the 3rd and 5th of a key sounded like, you would have known which two notes the guitarist played. What the interval was between the two notes is of little importance when trying to identify pitch. The important thing to realize from this example is that **all 12 pitches have a unique sound against a key and this unique sound can be memorized.**

Let's go back to our teacher again and explore another problem that comes from teaching intervals. The teacher tells the student that it may help them to memorize intervals if they relate the intervals to songs they know.   So the teacher suggests common melodies that they can use to help memorize these intervals, things like: a 4th is *Here Comes the Bride*, a 6th is *My Bonnie Lies over the Ocean*. So the student thinks "Wow this is great, now anytime I hear a 6th all I have to do is sing the first two notes of *My Bonnie Lies over the Ocean* and I'll know what notes are being played."

Once again let's look into this and explore two drawbacks of using common melodies to identify intervals:

1. The first two notes of *My Bonnie Lies over the Ocean* do comprise an interval of a 6th, but the 5th of the key up to the 3rd in the key is also a 6th.

Let's listen to this and see what happens when we play our "Bonnie 6th."

We're back on the bandstand playing a C chord vamp. The guitar player is playing the C chord with the bass playing a C, and the sax player plays a G (the fifth of the key) and then moves up to an E (the 3rd of the key) and you think "That's a sixth because I can hear that it is the beginning of *My Bonnie Lies over the Ocean*." Great! Now the sax player plays an Ab (the flat 6th of the key) and then moves up and plays an F (the 4th of the key). This is a sixth too, but can you easily hear *My Bonnie Lies over the Ocean* in this sound?

No.

This is because the first two notes of *My Bonnie Lies over the Ocean* are the 5th up to the 3rd of the key _not_ the flat 6th to the 4th. So once again **the important thing is to learn what each note sounds like in a key, _not_ what the distance is between notes.**

2. Let's say you're one of those students who has faithfully learned all your intervals and have developed the ability to grab a sound from any context and place an interval name on that sound by applying your memorized song to this interval.

All right— let's go back to our bandstand again and see how well it works as the band is jamming along.

Again the guitar player is playing the C chord with the bass playing a C and the sax player plays a G (the fifth of the key) and then moves up to an E (the 3rd of the key) the first thing that happens is you say to yourself "What is that sound I'm hearing," next you take that sound (the G up to E) and you run it through your mental rolodex of 11 basic intervals and the corresponding melodies that you have learned to identify these intervals. You come up with the correct answer and — Oops! The band is 2 bars past this point now and it's too late to use this information because it took you too long to calculate it. **Music moves by in time and the only relative pitch ear training that will help you is one that allows you the quickest identification of notes.**

Common Problems Associated with Ear Training

Let's also explore problems that creep up when students work on relative pitch ear training.

1. Our teacher plays a cadence I IV V I in the key of C which puts your "ear" into the key of C. Now the instructor plays an F. You immediately start singing up the scale from the root (C) to find the pitch the teacher is playing. You sing up to F and happily get the right answer. You get an "A+!"

But there's a problem here. Let's go back to our bandstand:

The guitar player is playing the C chord with the bass playing a C and the sax player plays an F (the fourth of the key) You now attempt to sing up the scale from the tonic that the bass and guitar are playing but whoa! Your guitarist has his double stack Marshall amplifier behind you with all knobs set on 11. You can't hear yourself sing up the scale to find out what pitch is being played.

So once again there's a problem. You can't rely on singing up to a note to identify it, you **just have to know by hearing the pitch what it's relationship is to a key.** I should also mention once again that by the time you have sung up the scale to find the pitch the band will have moved on, leaving you in the dust.

2. Here's another scenario: the teacher plays you a cadence I IV V I in the key of C which will put your "ear" into the key of C. Now the instructor plays an F#. You hear that this note exists outside of the key you have been set up to hear. (We say this note has *tension*.) When people encounter notes with these tensions, the common response is to resolve them, make them fit into the key (in this case, C) and then backtrack to name the note. F# commonly resolves up a half step to G so you now resolve the F# up in your mind to G which is the fifth. At that point you may be able to identify the G because you know the sound of the 5th of the key, or you may resolve the 5th down to the tonic or maybe you sing from the G note down the scale to C to get your answer. You may have finally gotten the correct answer but your method is flawed. First, you can't rely on resolution tendencies of notes because they don't always resolve the way you think they should when you place them in real music. Believe me, this resolution tendency will come back to haunt you later when you move on to two note ear training. And again, the time it takes for you to resolve this pitch in your mind is too long; you are in the dust once more.

So we are back to the fact that **You don't want to relate one pitch to another. You just want to know what each pitch sounds like in a key.**

Learning the Sound of Each Note

So how do we properly learn the sounds of all notes in a key? **Simply put, you need to memorize the sound of all 12 notes against a key center.** You can use no tricks. You must just listen to these notes over and over again until you start to internalize the unique sound of all 12 pitches against a key center. This is done two ways:

1. Listen to the Ear Training CD which will give you a cadence I IV V I in the key of C major. Each track will then playing a single note which you should trying to identify. Remember that you must listen to each note with the proper mind set. First realize that the only way this ear training will work in real time is for it to become instantaneous. You must hear a note and just <u>know</u> what that note is. When you start don't be afraid to guess if you don't know the answer. It is much better to guess than to try to use some trick or relate it to something extraneous in your mind. Eventually you will memorize the sounds of each of these notes, but it takes time and repeated listening before this happens. You will memorize these sounds more quickly if you listen to your Ear Training CD 4 or 5 times a day for 15 minutes rather than doing a one hour session. This is because by listening to the CD at many different times throughout a day you will keep the sounds fresh in your short term memory and this will help to entrench the information in your long term memory.

2. Singing pitches against a recurring tonal center such as a repeating major chord; that is, the tonic of the key. Notice I did not say singing *melodies*, I said singing *pitches*. One of the first errors a student makes when sight singing is that he or she will memorize the melody that a group of notes creates rather than learning what these notes sound like in the key. The human ear/mind has this ability to memorize a melody while having no idea what the pitches are or how they relate to a key. For the beginning student it is crucial to concentrate more on the sounds of each pitch rather than to memorize a melody. This will help develop an affinity with the sound of that pitch. When you sing an exercise you shouldn't just blindly move from one pitch to another, you should try to hear the pitch in your head before you sing it. If you find you aren't hearing it at first, don't worry, this will come with practice. If you don't hear the pitch you need in your head, just play it on an instrument so you can hear it. Always try to hear the pitch in your head first though, because this will start to develop the sound in your mind. Eventually you should be able to wean yourself away from the instrument. Many times students will also try to identify a pitch by the way it resonates in the throat. This is not recommended; you just have to learn what the pitch sounds like in your mind's ear and then sing it. I recommend "A Fanatic's Guide to Ear Training and Sight Reading" ISBN #189094419X for your singing exercises. The important thing is to have a recurring tonal center i.e. a repeating "one" chord sounding as you sing your pitches. The aforementioned book includes a CD for this purpose.

How to progress through each of the 3 Ear Training CDs

You should start with the Beginning CD. When you feel you are getting around 80% right you should move up to the Intermediate CD. When you feel you are getting around 80% right with the Intermediate CD start working with the advanced CD. When you feel like you are getting around 80% right you should move on to the "Key Note Recognition" book which will prepare you for the Ear Training Two Note Beginning Series of Books.

Ways to use the One Note Ear Training CD

The Ear Training CD works best if you use a CD player with shuffle play; this will guarantee that you don't memorize the order of the tracks. Many CD players especially those found in computerswill also allow you to choose which tracks you would like to hear. This is particularly helpful if you have problems with certain pitches or certain octaves. The One note CD series comes in three levels; beginning, intermediate, and advanced. Each CD in the series gets progressively faster so the listener has less time to respond with an answer. The order of notes and their corresponding octaves are found on the next page. This is useful if you want to make special sequences to work on particular pitches.

What Next?

Once you have mastered the advanced one note CD it's time to move on to the "Key Note Recogition" book and then the "Ear Training Two Note Beginning" Series. Visit http://www.muse-eek.com for details.

More Help

Muse Eek Publishing Company hosts two on-line resources in conjunction with this book. A "Frequently Asked Questions" page (FAQ) is available where students can ask the author questions that may arise as they work. There is also a free "member's section" where book owners can download other files specific to this book and/or other help files to further their music education.

Names of the Notes found on the Ear Training Beginning CD

1. D	34. C	67. B
2. A#	35. G	68. F#
3. F#	36. G	69. G
4. E	37. D#	70. E
5. B	38. A#	71. C#
6. A	39. C#	72. A
7. F	40. F#	73. G
8. C	41. G#	74. G#
9. F	42. E	75. A
10. G#	43. B	76. D
11. A	44. D	77. C
12. F#	45. B	78. A#
13. F	46. G	79. E
14. D#	47. G#	80. C
15. A#	48. B	81. A
16. A	49. D#	82. D#
17. F	50. F#	83. A#
18. E	51. C#	84. B
19. D#	52. F	85. B
20. G	53. G#	86. C
21. G#	54. B	87. D
22. F#	55. C#	88. A#
23. A	56. F#	89. D
24. C#	57. E	90. F
25. E	58. E	91. C#
26. A	59. C	92. B
27. F	60. G#	93. F
28. A#	61. C	94. F#
29. D	62. G	95. D#
30. C	63. G	96. C#
31. E	64. D	97. F
32. A	65. A#	98. G#
33. D#	66. D	99. D#

Names of the Notes found on the Intermediate Ear Training CD

1. E3	34. E2	67. E6
2. A3	35. A1	68. A5
3. A#2	36. A#4	69. F6
4. D4	37. G5	70. D#5
5. G3	38. C2	71. B6
6. C4	39. D1	72. G2
7. D#1	40. G#4	73. D1
8. B3	41. F#2	74. C3
9. F4	42. C#4	75. F5
10. F#1	43. F2	76. D#2
11. G#3	44. D#4	77. A#3
12. C#2	45. B1	78. F#1
13. B4	46. A#0	79. C#2
14. D#3	47. E5	80. G#4
15. F1	48. A2	81. B3
16. F#3	49. G#5	82. E4
17. G#1	50. F#5	83. A2
18. C#3	51. C7	84. F5
19. C1	52. G4	85. D#1
20. D3	53. D5	86. A#4
21. G1	54. A#1	87. G3
22. E4	55. A6	88. C2
23. A4	56. E1	89. D4
24. A#3	57. D#6	90. B1
25. D#2	58. F5	91. E2
26. B2	59. B0	92. A5
27. F3	60. C6	93. G#3
28. D2	61. G5	94. C#1
29. C3	62. D6	95. F#6
30. G2	63. G#1	96. B4
31. F#4	64. F#6	97. E1
32. G#2	65. C#5	98. A4
33. C#1	66. A#5	99. F1

Names of the Notes found on the Advanced Ear Training CD

1. F#	34. D	67. F
2. G	35. D	68. F#
3. F#	36. D#	69. G
4. G	37. A#	70. D#
5. A#	38. B	71. G#
6. A	39. F	72. D
7. E	40. G	73. A
8. C#	41. C	74. E
9. G#	42. D#	75. F
10. F#	43. E	76. D
11. B	44. C	77. F
12. E	45. A#	78. F
13. B	46. G	79. A
14. F#	47. C#	80. D
15. D	48. F	81. C#
16. A	49. F#	82. G#
17. G#	50. C	83. A#
18. C#	51. G#	84. E
19. B	52. A	85. A#
20. F#	53. D	86. E
21. A	54. E	87. C#
22. C	55. A	88. E
23. C	56. F	89. C#
24. A#	57. C	90. F
25. G	58. G#	91. D
26. A#	59. D#	92. A
27. F	60. G#	93. D#
28. B	61. G	94. B
29. E	62. C#	95. C
30. B	63. D#	96. F#
31. G	64. B	97. A#
32. G#	65. B	98. D#
33. A	66. D#	99. C

Frequently Asked Questions

It is strongly recommended that you read through these questions that various students have submitted. Although this method of ear training is simple in concept, tt is easy to do this ear training the wrong way either through previous misleasing musical training or just a misunderstanding on your part. If you don't proceed with this ear training with a good grasp of the concept, you will find that sooner or later you will hit a wall. Therefore, if you are not sure of some aspect PLEASE submit an FAQ to Muse Eek Publishing Company via the internet at FAQ@muse-eek.com or fax your question to 212-473-4601. It is of the highest priority us at Muse Eek Publishing Company that you fully understand all aspects of each of our method books. We have included questions pertaining to the "Ear Training One Note Series" and "The Fanatic's Guide to Ear Training and Sight Singing" because in many cases students are working out of both books and most of the time they are very closely related.

Some of the question found here relate to specifically to "The One Note Ear Training Series" or to "The Fanatic's Guide to Ear Training and Sight Singing" All have been included because proper development of ear training will only come by using a combination of listening and singing.

After I hear the progression and then the note on the CD, what am I listening for? Sometimes I find I can recognize the note because I remember a song that starts on that note. Is that OK?

When you first start this process of listening to the CD you should just be concerned with developing the proper response and not so much whether you are right or wrong. This can be hard for students to understand because they are used to attacking a problem with mental energy until they get the right answer. In this case the method you use to get the right answer is much more important than the right answer. Ear training only works well if you can do it in "real time." Music flows by in time so you need a quick response to make ear training useful. This is why developing the proper process is very important. Any process short of hearing a note and instantly recognizing that note will slow you down too much and make the ear training less and less useful. I commonly use the analogy of color. When you see someone with a blue shirt on you instantly know it's blue and it takes very little mental energy to come to this realization. The reason you can do this is because when you were a child you learned the colors by daily repetition in school, or in a family situation. There's no definition of the color blue just like there is no definition of what the 3rd of a key sounds like. You only gain the ability through repeated experience until your mind just remembers the color or the sound. So what are you listening for when you hear the note sound after the I IV V I progression? You aretrying to develop a recognition of what the note in question sounds like in relationship to the key. Each note has its own unique sound within a key and you are looking to memorize that sound through repetition. If you are recognizing notes because of a song you remember that is not a good idea for the following reasons. You have to go through the mental process of thinking, "Oh, I remember that note, it's the first note of this or that song." The time it takes to go through all that mental process will slow down your response time. Once again it's better to just hear the note and recognize it instantly because you have memorized its sound as it relates to the key.

I feel like I'm just wasting time. I use your method of listening to this CD, and I don't get any notes right and I'm just guessing what the note is.

Be patient. You have to understand that it will take time for you to memorize the sound of all twelve pitches against a key. Changing your attitude toward the listening will help you develop properly. Be more positive and remember that the learning process can be different for different things you are trying to learn. Learning sound is much more like learning a foreign language and is also closely related to how you learned color when you were a child-but no-one teaches you sound recognition in elementary school. Repetition and a positive attitude are crucial. You can try limiting the number of pitches you are working on. Program your CD to only play 3 or 4 different pitches. Most people find that they very quickly start to recognize these 3 or 4 pitches. But they also find when they go back to all twelve pitches they are right back to where they started; not getting the notes right. Keep in mind that remembering all these pitches can easily overload your analytical mind. So pace yourself and be constructive in you practicing. Most important once again is the process and that's why I recommend just guessing the note if you don't know it. You want an instant response and over time the correct answer will come.

After I hear the I IV V I progression I find that if I sing the tonic note in this case "C" it gives me more of a grounding in the key and I seem to get more pitches correct. Is this OK?

There are two possible reasons that the singing of the tonic helps you.

a. You have weak key retention so singing the note helps you keep the key
   in your short term memory. Unfortunately, singing the "C" can also keep your
   "key retention" weak because you start relying on the reinforcement of the key
   through your singing.

b. You are still using interval distance to tell what the note is and you use
   this reinforcement of the tonic "C" to help you judge the distance. A very counterproductive
   thing to do, because it is missing the whole point of memorizing the
   sound of each note against the key.

When I sing your exercises in the "Fanatic's Guide the Sight Singing and Ear Training" I sing out of tune a lot. Why does this happen?

There are a few reasons why this happens and it is very important to observe
yourself to find out why. Here are a few common reasons why this happens.

a. Rather than hearing what each note sounds like against the key center you
   are sliding your voice up or down to the next note and in reality you are trying to use
   the distance between the notes to calculate the next pitch rather than hearing what the
   desired pitch sounds like. This commonly makes people sing out of tune.

b. You have poor breath support. Make sure to take in enough air before
   singing each exercise. It is common to sing flat when you don't have enough breath to
   support the note.

c. You just don't know the sound of the note yet. As you get a strong concept
   of what each pitch sounds like you will find that you correct yourself because you hear
   that the pitch is not right.

I notice that all the listening for your "Ear Training: One Note Series" is in the key of C but the singing is done in all keys. Once you can do the listening in C, does it carry over to the other keys?

Yes, the 3rd of the key has the same "sound of the 3rd" in every key. It is important to realize that the sound of each note is the same in every key. By this I mean the 3rd always sounds like the 3rd. Therefore in the key of C major, E sounds like the 3rd. In the key of Ab major C sounds like the 3rd.

Does this type of ear training and sight singing only work with learning pieces that have a clear tonal center? What happens with "atonal" stuff?

All music and sound is in a key and therefore tonal. It just depends on your ability to hear these relationships, from Schoenberg to things that go bump in the night. If you have a well developed ear you will hear all music or sound in relationship to a key. You may not know the exact key if you aren't near a piano to figure it out, but as this ear training technique develops you will find music and sound taking on relative pitch assignments.

With the "Fanatic's Guide to Sight Singing and Ear Training" you say that a student should "sing each exercise starting on different pitches. For example C C# D would be Do Di Ra in C major but it would be Me Fa Fi in Ab major. Have the student sing these exercise from all 12 pitch levels." Do you mean play the I-IV-V-I in a variety of keys and find the same 3 pitches (c, c#, d) relative to each new key?

Yes, but I also have students sing Do, Di Ra in all keys just to make sure they are not using vocal placement to find the right pitch.

With the "Fanatic's Guide to Sight Singing and Ear Training" when you play the I-IV-V-I for singing, does it make any difference what inversion chords you play in the Right Hand? Is one easier/harder/preferable over another?

If you put the root in your left hand it will make no difference. I would recommend root position chords to begin with just to avoid any possible problems.

How has an improved ear changed your musicianship? My interest in this is twofold. First to be able to improvise and second, I have wondered if it would make the process of memorizing more efficient and reliable. Often, I can hear the sounds in my head but can't reliably identify the exact notes. Logically speaking, this type of earwork should enable me to know and find/play any note provided I can hear it in my head. Is this correct?

To answer your first question about improvisation:

By being able to hear what others are playing your improvisation is much more on target. Also there is a conscious/unconscious focusing of improvisational ideas because you can hear what notes you want to play and what their relationship is to the key of the moment.

To answer your 2nd question about identifying notes you hear in your head.

As you develop this ear training you will find that you are able to identify the notes your hear in your head because you can now put names to the notes you hear. This will make it much easier to catorgorize and memorize all musical sound.

The workbook specifies that you should learn the sound of all 12 pitches against a key and memorize the sounds. Yet the CD that comes with the workbook only has the key of C. Is this adequate to memorize the pitches against all keys?

You only need to memorize the sound of each pitch against one key because all keys have the same construction. (Remember, we are going for development of RELATIVE pitch, not perfect pitch!) For example the 3rd of every key sounds the same no matter what key you are in: An E sounds like the 3rd in the key of C while a C sounds like the 3rd in the key of Ab. I will mention that I do have students sing melodic exercises in all keys. This is mostly to counteract the frequent habit of memorizing the vocal placement of a note rather than truly hearing the sound of the note. I would highly recommend you work on singing melodic lines over a one chord drone along while working with the ear training CD. "A Fanatic's Guide to Ear Training and Sight Singing" ISBN 189094419X is an excellent source for melodies but also explains the proper way to approach this singing.

I am a mostly self-taught musician with a good grounding in the rudiments of musical theory, and I have done a bit of formal ear training (traditional interval instruction) as well; so I'm obviously not a beginner, but which book would you recommend I buy - "One Note Intermediate Level" or "Advanced?" I can sight-sing simple melodies in the treble and bass clefs and identify simple triads when I hear them with ease. What do you think?

I would recommend you get the Intermediate level. Let me explain that all three books are essentially the same text; what changes is the content of the CDs that come with the books. The CDs contain aural exercises, and how quickly you hear the note and how quickly the answer is given, from CD to CD, is what changes. The CDs are designed to convey a method for developing fast and accurate answers to this specific type of ear training so I recommend not starting out with the advanced level because it won't give you enough time to think of the answer in the right way. As long as we are on the subject of how to do this ear training correctly I should recommend two new books "A Fanatic's Guide to Ear Training and Sight Singing" (which is an excellent resource for Sight Singing) and "Key Note Recognition" which is another Ear Training CD to help with identifying key centers. These could both be very useful to you. When I have my private students work with the CDs and the exercises found in these books I find they have great success.

I just received Book One of ear training. In the CD you provide a I-IV-V-I cadence followed by a note to identify. For example, the first note you play on track 1 is D. Well, what about the key of your chord progression? If your chord progression is in the key of C, then D sounds like a major second. However, if your chord progression is in the key of G, then the D sounds like a perfect fifth. Without knowing the key of your chord progression, the best I can hope for is to say that the note sounds like a 2nd or a flat 5, etc. It seems that to understand relative pitch, which is what you are suggesting I learn, I must know the key of the progression. I can't simply hear a I-IV-V-I cadence and then you play a note and expect me to give you the pitch. That would require that I have perfect, not relative pitch ear training. I would appreciate your thoughts.

The Ear Training CD gives you a I-IV-V-I cadence in the key of C. I overlooked mentioning that the all exercises on the CD are in the key of C Major, although I think it would become apparent to you after a while. But thanks for pointing it out; because of your feedback I am now putting stickers on the CDs to make this clear. Your other observations about this type of ear training are correct. I hope you find this method as helpful as my students have.

I would appreciate some clarification about your ear training CDs. I hope you can take a minute to give me some encouragement. I am an adult amateur singer in a community chorus and am gradually improving my skills through private voice lessons and self study. Recently I bought your "Ear Training — One Note Beginning Level". The concept is intriguing, and in accord with my own perception of ear-training. Learning intervals by association with popular songs does not seem terribly useful to me. Our chorus has been working on sight-singing with movable-do solfege. This has been useful and seems like a good approach. I find the idea of recognizing notes in their relation to a key much more attractive than learning intervals in the abstract. However, your recording takes pitch recognition to a new level. The exercises are quite overwhelming. I mostly feel that I am guessing the pitch. Occasionally, I feel a sense of certainty and get one right, but I'm not sure I'm doing better than the 1 in 12 that I would get by pure chance. It's hard to see that the practice would ever lead to improvement; it feels so hopeless at first. I admit that I have not put much effort into this project, since success seems so far away. Is this a typical experience? Do beginning students usually report the sort of frustration that I am reporting — and then find that they eventually improve? When your text is used in college music programs, what sort of practice regimen is expected? I would be grateful for any clarification or encouragement you can give me.

Your feeling of hopelessness is common among many beginners to this ear training method. Many of my students initially feel that they are guessing so much that they feel like it's mostly random guessing and they are only getting the notes right by luck.

But don't let it get you down. There IS a method in this madness. The reason for the guessing is to ensure you don't start to manufacture a mental set of hoops you jump through to get a note right. For instance, students will start singing down to the tonic with whatever note they are listening to. This is one of many crutches that students use. The problem is music goes by in real time so you need to have an instant recognition of the sound. By guessing the first thing that comes into your mind you are setting up the proper response mechanism. So, really it's not important in the beginning to get the note right, it's important to "do it right" to set up a habit of "how you answer."

The next problem of course is how to get the notes right. The process of learning the sound of each pitch against a key center employs a learning technique that you haven't probably used since you were a child. Think back on how you learned about colors as a child. There is no definition of the color Blue just as there is no definition of what the 3rd of a key sounds like. You just have to see the color blue over and over again until you remember what it looks like. It is the same for this ear training. You hear these notes over and over again— hopefully many times a day, and you continue to guess until you start to remember the sounds. It usually takes students a while to get used to this type of learning again. Be patient with yourself.

The other side of this is to also work on singing exercises. Students that combine singing exercises along with the listening to the One Note CDs improve A LOT quicker. I recommend the "Fanatic's Guide to Sight Singing and Ear Training." If you do a combination of both books each day I think you will find your improvement will accelerate.

Really one of the secrets here is that if you listen to the One Note CD and sing exercises out of the Fanatic's Guide each day you are consistently keeping the sounds of these notes in your short term memory. Sooner or later these sounds will go into your permanent memory. Therefore the more you can do the listening and singing each day the faster you will improve. Your listening and singing sessions do not have to be long (5-10 minutes) but the important thing is to do this at least 3 times a day and hopefully 10 times a day. As I have mentioned, doing the ear training many times a day in short intervals will help your short term memory keep these sounds in your head. Sooner or later your short term memory will pass this over to your permanent memory and then you will just know a sound when you hear it.

I recommend to my students to do the One Note CD while riding in a car, train, plane or any place that you have a little extra down time. The singing is a little trickier. But be creative and find ways to do a quick Fanatic's Guide exercise at lunch or breaks at work.

When you say that you haven't really worked at the technique that much because you feel so daunted, remember, if you don't do it, you'll never get it, and then your doubts will become a self-fulfilling prophecy.

In closing EVERYONE that has studied this ear training has been able to do it. For some it came very quickly (a couple of weeks) for most it takes 6 months to a year. For others it can be a 3-5 year tortured experience. But if you talk to the most tortured you will find they all say it was worth it because to just hear notes and know what they are puts you so close to music and puts your ability to function as a musician on a whole different level. If you end up getting the Fanatic's Guide write back and I'll assign you a few exercises to get you started. In the meantime keep the faith, you will get this right it just takes time and I'm here for encouragement if you need it.

I understand that you feel the traditional interval-based ear training to be impractical. I've never done any extensive ear training before. After trying your method for about a month, I noticed that it actually worked, but in a very specific, limited way. When I listen to a piece of music, first I need to hear the key. Naturally, I don't need to identify what key it is, but I need to get a sense of the key, whatever it is. Based on your ear training, until I get a sense of the key, I cannot identify anything. The problem with this is that much of the modern music (pop, jazz, dance, electronic, rap, etc..) has very vague use of key. Even with very straight forward pop songs, many of them would not establish any key until the chorus section. Some songs don't at all for the entire song. Some songs are modal and get very confusing as to how to interpret the key. The keys for many pieces of music are a matter of interpretation. When I cannot establish a key in my mind, I find that I can't use what I've learned in your ear training. It only works with old classical music like Bach, or very elementary pop music like Britney Spears.

Thanks for contacting me and asking such excellent questions. First let me say that your progress is great for only working with one of the Ear Training One Note books for a month. It's great that you are applying your ear training to "real" music. First let me discuss some general topics so you can understand my overall beliefs concerning ear training.

I don't believe there is such a thing as Atonal music. All sound has a pitch and as sound groups together it forms a key. If your ears are good enough you will be able to distinguish this key center. Of course you will need a reference pitch which people usually get from the instrument they are playing. I should point out that many times in supposed "atonal music" the key centers are changing very quickly. These quickly changing keys require you to learn how to modulate which is what the Ear Training: Two Note Series starts to teach you. Anton Webern one of the fathers of this supposed "atonal music" explains in the book THE PATH TO THE NEW MUSIC, PUBLISHER (Bryn Mawr, Pa., T. Presser Co. [c1975]) that he doesn't believe that there is such a thing as "atonal" music. His reasoning falls along the same lines as mine. Arnold Schoenberg has also been quoted as believing that no music is "atonal" and hated the reference of "atonal" to his music and others. Both these composers felt that you could hear the key centers moving in highly chromatic music or even music created using 12 tone rows. I should interject at this point that getting to the point where you hear for example Schoenberg's Funf Klavierstucke (Five Piano Pieces Opus 23) in a key or quickly moving keys will not happen in a month of ear training. It will happen though, after years of working with this method.

Your statement "The problem with this (the ear training method) is that much of the modern music (pop, jazz, dance, electronic, rap, etc..) has very vague use of key" I do agree that many styles of contemporary music have a vague sense of key when you compare it with Mozart. But you will find that this ear training method will eventually help you develop better skills in hearing keys in this type of music. Let's examine how you should proceed to reach this level of proficiency.

There are two sides to practicing this ear training method. One is listening to the CDs, the other is doing singing exercises. For the listening you should progress through the books in the following sequence:

1. Ear Training: Beginning to Intermediate to Advanced

2. Key Note Recognition

3. The Two Note Series.

Note: After the two notes series you need to move to 3, 4, 5 notes at a time. At this writing I haven't finished books for these levels though they are in the works (02/01/01)

For Singing I recommend starting with "The Fanatic's Guide to Ear Training and Sight Singing." You would then continue with:

1. Lines: Sight Singing and Sight Reading Exercises

2. Specific studies out of other books, like "Single String Studies Volumes One and Two,"

3. Singing along with chord progressions and melodies from modern repertory pieces like jazz standards, pop, jazz, dance, electronic, rap, etc..)

This should give you a general idea of the progression through this ear training method. Obviously you will need to interact with me so that I can lead you through all of this. But in general I would follow the path I set out for you above. Of course if you have any questions please contact me. The worst thing you can do is work on any of this ear training the wrong way. I feel I have explained it pretty well in the books but if you're not sure please check with me first.

I should also mention that you could use your method of just transcribing melodies using only the interval relationship, but my objections to this method are as follows.

1. This method obviously divorces you from what key these pitches are functioning in. It's a bit like "follow the dots." You may end up with an outline that looks like something, but there will not be any sense of the underlying form that holds it all together and gives it shape. When I store melodies in my memory, I store them as they relate to the key, not as how the individual notes relate to each other.

2. After working with intervals, most students have extreme difficulty developing the proper technique when doing the Ear Training Two Note (+) method.

3. In the improvisational/interactive setting of a band, if someone is playing constant sixteenth notes at quarter note equals 80, you are far better off knowing the key that these notes are functioning in than knowing the actual pitches. If you can hear the key you can interact in a creative way with the other musicians.

4. As you develop through the ear training method presented in my books you will find that your ability to transcribe anything will improve exponentially. Give it a chance and you will see.

Hope this helps you understand the method better.

Why do you emphasize thinking and singing individual pitches as opposed to melodic line?

We have the ability to memorize melodies and have absolutely no idea what pitches we are singing. Go to a baseball game and listen to the National Anthem. Do these people know what notes they are singing? By singing individual pitches and keeping away from hearing these pitches as part of a melodic pattern you focus on what the sound of each pitch is, as opposed to memorizing a melody.

I'm working with your ear training method. It's a very fun book to work with 'cause I had the cd always in the car and practice every day for about 20 minutes. I nearly get right about 80% of the notes but I'm not sure if I am doing this right or not. Sometimes I hear the note from the key chord but other times I know that I recognize the note by memory (a particular note relates to a particular tune for example). How do I know when I'm doing it the right way? (I started the book a week ago)

I'm glad you have been working on the books. As far as the ear training goes, what you are aiming for is the ability to just hear a note and instantly recognize its sound. It's like when you see a person with a blue shirt on. You just instantly know it's blue you don't have to compare it to the sky to make sure. It is the same with the ear training.

You also mention that you recognize the note based on another common melody you know. I don't recommend that because if you have to take the time to relate the note you are hearing to a tune it just takes too much time. Remember you are trying to get to the point where you can do this ear training in real time as music is being played. In real time situations you won't have time to think of anything but what the note is.

How have your students found their musical ability changes after developing this ear training method?

My students have found that this ear training totally changes their abilities as musicians and is a real springboard for their artistic expression. Some students develop this type of ear training very quickly while others take months or years. Much of this variation in the amount of time it takes students to develop this style of ear training depends on their commitment to practicing and on their prior ear training habits. One of the reasons for making a document like this available is to help students with problems identify what they are doing wrong, so their studies will proceed more quickly.

I have a couple of questions about using this approach to ear training (which I'm in the process of trying). Firstly, do I simply keep listening & guessing? What if my guesses are completely wrong? Do I take a Zen-like attitude & simply persevere, mindless of success & failure? Secondly, & somewhat related to the first query, is it advisable to train on a subset of the various keynote relationships? For example training using just notes E & G, say against C Major?

Thanks for purchasing Ear Training One Note. To answer your first question:
Yes, just keep guessing. First, you want to build up the proper response in your mind. This is basically

1. I hear a note
2. I ask myself what is that note
3. I answer with the first thing that comes into my mind

Over time you will find that you start to remember what these notes sound like and your success rate will improve. Many of my students have found that if they do short intervals of practice from 5-15 minutes 5 or 6 times a day they improve at a quicker rate. This is because you keep the sounds of the notes in your short term memory better when you reinforce it many times throughout the day. As your short term memory of these notes improves, sooner or later this will move over to your permanent memory.

You also might want to go to the "members area" of the muse-eek.com website and download the Ear Training file. This will give you more information about how to approach this technique. I should also mention that when I teach this method of ear training I also have students working on singing these pitches too. I find this helps with their progress. I use "The Fanatics Guide to Ear Training and Sight Singing."

To answer your second question. Yes, you can use subsets to help you focus in on a couple of notes at a time. The way the CD is set up really helps this process. Many students use their computer for this so they can save the subset lists for future use.

I think you also should keep in mind that in my experience every student that has stuck with this method eventually gets it. Depending on your background this can take a week or a few years. For me it was the latter, unfortunately, but the difference this made in my musical ability made it well worth the time and effort. (It also made me very sensitive to just how hard it is for some people to do it.)

You should start thinking about Ear Training as a life long pursuit and not something that you will do for a while and then stop. I still work on this ear training every day. It's around 22 years now that I have been doing this type of ear training. Of course I'm working on much harder and more complicated exercises than the One Note ear training. But it is all based on the basic concept of hearing what each pitch sounds like against a key.

Your reference to Zen while humorous, is not without relevance. The kind of patience and delight in process (being IN the action, not focusing on the results of the action) that Zen promotes can be helpful to you in this situation, by eliminating frustration.

I am a guitarist, and have been playing for 3 years. I am reasonably good, but what is holding me back is my musical ear. Improvisation, and working out songs off a cd is extremely difficult for me. I do not think I am tone-deaf, but my musical ear is very restricted. If I was tone deaf, would your course still help, or is it a lost cause? I am seriously considering buying your course books for ear training. What books of yours should I use with them? How will I know if the course is working? And is it difficult too follow? I hope the course is simple to understand and use. What state of relative pitch can your courses make me achieve? Is it possible to get amazing relative pitch from your courses? Or does it just enable me to get average relative pitch. Also, is it possible to develop perfect pitch? If so, do you have any courses dealing with that, or know any good courses you can recommend for me. Thanks a lot,

First, I applaud you for your realization that you should do something about your weakness in aural perception. Many players don't even address this aspect of their musicianship. I have been teaching for 21 years and have never met anyone who is tone-deaf. Literally if you were tone deaf you wouldn't be able to distinguish music for any other sound. It would all sound mono chromatic with no variance in pitch. What has most likely happened to you is your mind has never latched on to a system for identifying pitches so it doesn't know how to process the sound when it hears it.

So the next step is to teach your mind how to recognize sound in a way that will allow you to hear what others are playing in person or on record. You also want to develop the ability to know what you hear inside your head so you can compose and improvise. This is a long process and doesn't have a quick fix. By using a combination of the books I've written along with dedication and perseverance, you can conquer this problem. It's also going to be very frustrating when you start working in these books because you are not going to get the answers correct for a while, so you will have to be patient and believe in yourself and that you can accomplish your goal.

I would start with buying two books, Ear Training: One Note Beginning and Fanatic's Guide to Ear Training and Sight Singing. Read and reread the introductions to these books. I can't stress how important it is for you to work on the ear training the correct way. It is very easy to try and find short cuts with the process that will only screw you up in the long run. Also, after you've purchased a book, join the "member's area" on the muse-eek.com website and read the article I've posted there on ear training. If you have further questions on how to organize your practice, write back and I'll give you a practice regimen tailored to your needs.

For your question about the Beatles: I think they were the most important figures in 20th century popular music. Their influence on musicians and listeners eclipsed all other pop artists.

What is your recommendation for combining the Ear Training and Fanatic's aural exercises? Do you alternate lessons from each book daily or do you have another method that will maximize results? Thanks for your time and I am looking forward to hearing better.

Thanks for contacting me. I'm glad you have both the Fanatic's Guide and an Ear Training One Note book (I assume it's a one note book.) Working on both singing and listening is very important to fast progress. One of the key ingredients to improving at the fastest pace with this method is to practice several times throughout the day, as opposed to one long session. 15-20 twenty minute intervals would be ideal. During this practice time you should work in both books by listening to the CD for the One Note Book and then doing some of the singing exercises out of the Fanatic's Guide. Make sure you always use the Fanatic's Guide CD with any exercise you sing. It is important to always hear your voice in relation to a key center.

Another main ingredient is your understanding of what you are trying to do inside your head with this ear training and how you deal with your own preconceptions and old habits. These questions are usually dealt with by me in a private lesson over a period of time. In this case we don't have that luxury. To deal with this problem I have written a 10 page article that is free for you because you own a muse-eek book. You can find this article in the "member's area" of the muse-eek.com website. This article will give you much more information on how to approach each book and the how's and why's of organizing your practice time. I think you would greatly benefit from reading this information before you start into this ear training method. It may also create some more specific questions relating to your take on the process.

Remember you are trying to reprogram the way you hear music. If you start to think about that it's a pretty massive task. Luckily this method will do this for you BUT you need to be fully involved in monitoring and analyzing your practice habits and your perception of sound.

It is important that you read the FAQs under all the ear training books on the muse-eek.com website. In theory this ear training method is simple, yet once your mind starts to process sound and you are in the middle of practicing you'd be surprised how many different right and wrong perceptions students have of what is the "right thing to do."

Let me know if you have any more questions and I wish you good luck with your progress.

I understand your approach to ear training and I believe it will work in my case. For example, I could never figure out how to superimpose the sound of a minor 3rd when trying to sing from a 3rd degree to a 5th degree in a key. I just knew the sound of the 5th degree and sang it re-gardless of what note I was coming from. Of course I always thought this approach must be wrong (i.e. not using the sound of the interval) and tried to resist it. Now that you've given me the okay to do it this way, my sight-singing has DRASTICALLY improved (in only a few short weeks).

Anyway, my question is at what point in this process will I begin to hear and understand (immediately) short melodies. After all, that is what the music is all about and what I'm ulti-mately trying to reproduce (either by singing or playing my instrument)?

The ability to apply this ear training method in "real life" varies for each person. For me it took about 6 months before I first started to hear a few notes here and there. These were usually over a drone and at a very slow tempo. Of course this all depends on how quickly you develop with this ear training. I was very slow but then again, I've had many students get "one note" ear training in 2 weeks—then they start to apply it right away— much quicker than my 6 months. To get a more drastic perspective, other students with a real weakness can take 4 years to just get "one note" ear training. Of course to some people that seems like "forever." But, I can tell you that all these stu-dents experience a profound difference in their musicianship after they start to hear correctly. They not only can hear what notes are played but they play so much more musically, that there is no comparison.

I've also noticed that some students can get "one note" ear training on the CDs OK but it takes them much longer to apply this to real life playing situations. I believe a lot of this depends on whether a person tries to apply it, or whether they compartmentalize the exercises into an isolated academic study. Again, for some musicians it takes time for them to integrate this new ear training technique into their everyday interaction with music.

From your description of how your are singing the notes it sounds like you are on the right track. I hope you are working with both a "one note" book and the Fanatic's Guide. By doing both singing and listening exercises you will improve at the fastest rate.

First of all I would like to thank you for everything you have done for me. The effort you have put into helping other people out is fantastic. I printed off the ear training document in the members area, and I would like to thank you for taking to the time to do that so that I, and many people like me, can benefit.

When reading how the process of learning works, I got quite confused. Are the books very simple to understand? I have good theory knowledge, I am doing grade five theory, I don't know if that is the same system used in America, but in Australia there are seven grades and I'm doing grade five. I hope that gives you some idea of where I am up to. It is not the theory I don't understand, more the way to use your exercises and the process that I learn by.

There are some more questions I would really like some answers to as well. I really hope this doesn't sound rude, but I really want to hear from you that your books really do work. If you could tell me wether you know for a fact you have had proven results from the books that would be great. I am going to start learning from your books, and I am going to dedicate a lot of time, so hearing from you that results are achievable will really motivate me. I read some-where that it took you personally 1 and a half years to get the tone recognition your books teach. Is that a correct statement? And where did you learn it from? Because my musical ear is quite weak does that mean it will take me longer to get the exercises? Another question I would like answered is wether you know if perfect pitch is learnable or not. Do you have to be born with it, or can it be learned? Have you heard of the David Burge's perfect pitch course? What do you think of that if you know of it? I was considering buying that course, but for some reason I believed your course would be better for me.

I don't know whether you would be able to answer this question, but how come some people have excellent relative pitch without any training? I don't see how they could know everything that your course teaches without hearing anything from your course? Will I develop the same awareness as them over time, or will the awareness I develop be memory based, whereas their awareness is kind of built into their brain. An answer to that question would really be great, I hope you understand what I'm talking about. What is the difference between the two note and one note series? Will your course help me recognize chord progressions such as I VIm V VII I? will it also help me hear a guitar riff then reproduce it perfectly? Will it help me hear wether something is in key or not?

I found a computer ear training program called earmaster 4. The program had a note recogni-tion exercise where a I IV V I progression was played, and I got very little right. The ones I did get right were probably guesses. I found it very hard, and don't see how my ear could learn to recognize any of the pitches. It would be great if you could take the time to answer all the questions in my e-mail. I know there are a lot, and I'm sorry that there are so many, but they are all important to me.

I also going to order the "Fanatics Guide" that you suggested very soon, in the next two or three days. Thank you so much once again for everything you have done for me. It is great the amount of student teacher interaction you provide, and I have been telling lots of people about your course.

Thanks again for everything, and I look forward to hearing from you again.

Well you do have a lot of questions don't you. It is actually great that you do. It shows you really want to be positive in your mind that you are doing the ear training correctly. I wish more students were that inquisitive. Before I get into your questions let me just say that learning ear training is like learning any new subject. You start out thinking you understand what to do and what is the correct path and usually along the way as you understand the subject more you realize that some of the things you thought were correct when you started actually turn out to be incorrect. Think about this, the most important thing you can do as you progress through this ear training is to question yourself to make sure you aren't taking short cuts and are really following the process correctly. The process is simple:

You hear a progression that puts you musical mind in a key center
You hear a note
You listen to that note
you say to yourself what does that note sound like
If you think you have the answer "say it"
If you don't know, guess.
Over time you will get the right answer because sooner or later your mind will remember the sounds of these notes as they relate to the key center.

That said, let's look at your questions.

I believe the books are easy to understand but I've also found that whether a student is using the books or has private instruction from me, they still occasionally have problems. That's because there are so many possibilities regarding exactly how they approach the process, that problems and questions can arise.

As far as your music theory knowledge goes. If you know what all 12 chromatic notes are in the key of C major you are ready to do the one note ear training. The Fanatic's Guide will require you to know the same information in all keys. BUT, you can actually use the Fanatic's Guide to help you develop your theoretical knowledge of all keys by working through specific exercises to help you build your internal theoretical knowledge.

To reiterate: as far as how to work through the exercises in the One Note Ear Training books: you want to listen to the progression, hear a note and guess what it is. If you don't know what the note is just guess, that is completely OK to do this. Think back on how you learned about colors as a child. There is no definition of the color Blue just as there is no definition of what the 3rd of a key sounds like. You just have to see the color blue over and over again until you remember what it looks like. It is the same for this ear training. You hear these notes over and over again— hopefully many times a day, and you continue to guess until you start to remember the sounds. By also working with the Fanatic's Guide and singing these pitches you will find that over time you will remember the sound. As I have mentioned, doing the ear training many times a day in short intervals will help your short term memory keep these sounds in your head. Sooner or later your short term memory will pass this over to your permanent memory and then you will just know a sound when you hear it.

As far as the books go. Yes, they do actually work, I have had many students who "got" the relative pitch. That's why I wrote the books. But it requires you to read and reread all the information I have posted and sent you about this subject. It requires that you work everyday on the ear training and only miss a day in the advent of a nuclear explosion. You need to be very diligent about doing this especially if you are very weak at ear training. My teacher used to say if you miss a day when you are starting out it's like missing 3 weeks .

It took me a year and half to get one note. Most of my students do not have that problem mostly because of all the books I have available (—and also because I am a slave driver....). I didn't have these so it took longer. Also I had a lot of "interval training" before I started this method of ear training and it took me a long time to unlearn hearing by interval and just recognize the pitch against a key center. I have had students that couldn't tell which pitch was higher or lower when the pitches were 2 to 3 octaves apart and they "got" this ear training —though in that case it took about 3 years. BUT, they also didn't work on it as much as they should have.

I learned part of this ear training method from a wonderful teacher in Boston by the name of Charlie Banacos. Other parts of the ear training I learned from teachers at Berklee College of Music or Jerry Bergonzi another wonderful instructor in the Boston area.

It is hard to say how long it will take you to "get one note." I will say that you should stop thinking about how weak your ear is and just concentrate on making it better. EVERYONE gets this ear training that tries. EVERYONE has weaknesses in life and it's the ones who persevere that make it.

Having the aural capacity to distinguish notes isn't something people are born with. BUT, if you grow up and learn the sound of each note within a key 'instinctively,' (usually this "natural" method was helped "just a bit" by their music teacher or parents that are musicians though few will admit it.) You will of course have what seems like a gift from God. I've taught thousands of students over the last 20+ years and I've never had a student that had a "Gift from God." I've had students that could do the one note ear training in a week or two but once we progress into two notes and more, they soon reach their peak and have to work like everyone else. By the way, all ear training ability is "memory based." Your ability will not be any different from the supposed "natural" talent. Your mind learns by first placing sound in your short term memory and then over time it enters your permanent memory. These folks you speak of just have the ear training in their permanent memory as you will too, as you develop.

As far as your question about the differences between one note and two note + ear training. I think you should get a handle on one note ear training first. I see no benefit in trying to make you understand the two note ear training method now. You're asking how to run before you can walk. I will say that you will definitely have to master two or more note ear training before you are going to sit there and know you are hearing "I VIm V VII I." You will find though that as you gain control of one note ear training you will start to quickly hear what key a song or chord progression is in and you will also start to recognize the pitches contained in simple melodies.

Perfect pitch is learnable. But I think relative pitch is much more useful for a performing and improvising musician than perfect pitch. Mr. Burge's method has it's problems though. It's on the right track as far a method goes but doesn't cover all of the ways that perfect pitch can be taught so I would guess this would make the process much harder for some individuals. The way you "hear" notes in a perfect pitch method is completely different from relative pitch, so I don't think this would be a method for you to start working on right now.

I have a question about natural talent. From the things I've read it seems like you don't believe that there is such thing, but what about Mozart? He had naturally amazing musical ear. And my friend who has good relative pitch wasn't born with a naturally good ear, how did he get it from just playing music?

Mozart was taught by his father from a <u>very</u> early age. It's obvious that he "thought" of music and sound the "right way" very quickly. I'm sure some of this was just the "natural" way he saw the world. BUT, lets say he grew up with a father that was a farmer, and he never had an instrument or lessons as a child, and was never pushed VERY hard by his father or given time to practice and develop. If we stopped him in the fields when he was 25 years old and said write an opera called "The Magic Flute" would he be able to do it? I doubt it.

As I said before:

"Having the aural capacity to distinguish notes isn't something people are born with. BUT, if you grow up and learn the sound of each note within a key 'instinctively,' You will of course have what seems like a gift from God. I've taught thousands of students over the last 20+ years and I've never had a student that had a "Gift from God."

But really the main thing is you shouldn't waste your time pondering these irrelevant thoughts, possibilities, and situations. If you practice the right thing you can be as good as anyone. For some people though, the amount of practice needed to become a great musician may be more than they are willing to give. It that case they should do something else. If you personally don't have the patience and the dedication to correct the musicianship problems you have then you shouldn't be involved in music. -and certainly not pondering your relative relationship to Mozart—a genius who ate, breathed, and lived music most of his waking hours.

I've been working with the one note intermediate CD for about six weeks. I am a trained musician with a music degree (Guitar performance,Berklee class of '79) and was astonished and humbled by how weak my ear was. What a reality check! I am really pleased with your materials (wish I had done this way back when, instead of the largely ineffective methods I was taught). I have a couple of questions. Having read the website, my understanding is that if I am hearing non diatonic tones with even the slightest sense of them resolving to diatonic tones then I have more work to do. Is this a correct impression? I'm afraid that my previous training has me at a disadvantage to even a rank beginner because I must "unlearn" the way I was taught in order to improve. I have ordered the one note advanced level and need to know whether I should move on or stay with the intermediate until all problems are solved. I am currently about 92-93% accurate on average, never dipping below 90%. In fact, the only real issue I seem to have is with the highest A, B, and C (last three white keys on the piano). I don't have problems with these notes in any other octave, but I hear those three almost more as noises than identifiable pitches. Perhaps years of loud gigging have taken their toll (I'm 46). Is this a common problem? Am I not giving those last three notes enough time? Should I move on to the next level? I am determined to finally bring this aspect of my musicianship up to as high a level as I can possibly achieve and am willing to devote as many years as it takes to "free-up" my ear. Hopefully you can shed some light on my questions. Thanks in advance.

Thanks for contacting me. Looks like we actually went to school together. I was at Berklee from 1978 to 1980. It's funny how some concepts get past even the best schools. I really feel that it would have had a major impact on me as a freshman in college if I would have known to work on this type of ear training. I too had to unlearn many things I was taught about ear training and other aspects of music in order to continue to evolve as a musician. It took me a year and a half to unlearn interval training so I could then start to hear how notes sound against a key center.

Given enough time, your perception sharpens and things like resolution tendencies of notes take their proper place in your mind. Each person is different of course but it sounds like from your description that you are ready to work on the advanced level of the one note ear training. You need to continue to make a mental effort to base your answers on how the note sounds in a key and not its resolution tendency. As I'm sure you realize a #4 doesn't always resolve to the 5th so it makes no sense to use that as method of identifying the #4.

The problem you are having with the very high notes is common. You will find that eventually your perception will get sharper and these notes will come into to focus better. I also highly recommend that you work with the CDs in the "One Note Ear Training" books along with doing singing exercises from the "Fanatic's Guide to Ear Training and Sight Singing." By working on your ear training from both angles your progress will be much faster. You can check the Muse-eek.com "member's area" for some specific lessons to start with in this book. Or just use the suggested methods in the book. Overall I think it is important for you to realize that the people who do the best with this ear training are those who make a long term commitment to improving their aural perception of sound. With the attitude that you can always be better than you are, you will find that your understanding of music will consistantly grow and evolve. I have stuck with this ear training now for almost 20 years and the understanding of sound this has provided me has been worth every minute of work I put into it.

Please see the muse-eek.com website for more FAQs and check back evey month for updates.

Books Available From
Muse Eek Publishing Company

The Bruce Arnold series of instruction books for guitar are the result of 20 years of teaching. Mr. Arnold, who teaches at New York University and Princeton University has listened to the questions and problems of his students, and written forty books addressing the needs of the beginning to advanced student. Written in a direct, friendly and practical manner, each book is structured in such as way as to enable a student to understand, retain and apply musical information. In short, these books teach.

1st Steps for a Beginning Guitarist
Spiral Bound ISBN 1890944-90-4   Perfect Bound ISBN 1890944-93-9

"1st Steps for a Beginning Guitarist" is a comprehensive method for guitar students who have no prior musical training. Whether you are playing acoustic, electric or twelve-string guitar, this book will give you the information you need, and trouble shoot the various pitfalls that can hinder the self-taught musician. Includes pictures, videos and audio in the form of midifiles and mp3's.

Chord Workbook for Guitar Volume 1 (2nd edition)
Spiral Bound ISBN 0-9648632-1-9   Perfect Bound ISBN 1890944-50-5

A consistent seller, this book addresses the needs of the beginning through intermediate student. The beginning student will learn chords on the guitar, and a section is also included to help learn the basics of music theory. Progressions are provided to help the student apply these chords to common sequences. The more advanced student will find the reharmonization section to be an invaluable resource of harmonic choices. Information is given through musical notation as well as tablature.

Chord Workbook for Guitar Volume 2 (2nd edition)
Spiral Bound ISBN 0-9648632-3-5   Perfect Bound ISBN 1890944-51-3

This book is the Rosetta Stone of pop/jazz chords, and is geared to the intermediate to advanced student. These are the chords that any serious student bent on a musical career must know. Unlike other books which simply give examples of isolated chords, this unique book provides a comprehensive series of progressions and chord combinations which are immediately applicable to both composition and performance.

Music Theory Workbook for Guitar Series

The world's most popular instrument, the guitar, is not taught in our public schools. In addition, it is one of the hardest on which to learn the basics of music. As a result, it is frequently difficult for the serious guitarist to get a firm foundation in theory.

Theory Workbook for Guitar Volume 1
Spiral Bound ISBN 0-9648632-4-3   Perfect Bound ISBN 1890944-52-1

This book provides real hands-on application of intervals and chords. A theory section written in concise and easy to understand language prepares the student for all exercises. Worksheets are given that quiz a student about intervals and chord construction using staff notation and guitar tablature. Answers are supplied in the back of the book enabling a student to work without a teacher.

Theory Workbook for Guitar Volume 2
Spiral Bound ISBN 0-9648632-5-1   Perfect Bound ISBN 1890944-53-X

This book provides real hands-on application for 22 different scale types. A theory section written in concise and easy to understand language prepares the student for all exercises. Worksheets are given that quiz a student about scale construction using staff notation and guitar tablature. Answers are supplied in the back of the book enabling a student to work without a teacher. Audio files are also available on the muse-eek.com website to facilitate practice and improvisation with all the scales presented.

Rhythm Book Series

These books are a breakthrough in music instruction, using the internet as a teaching tool! Audio files of all the exercises are easily downloaded from the internet.

Rhythm Primer
Spiral Bound ISBN 0-890944-03-3   Perfect Bound ISBN 1890944-59-9

This 61 page book concentrates on all basic rhythms using four rhythmic levels. All examples use one pitch, allowing the student to focus completely on time and rhythm. All exercises can be downloaded from the internet to facilitate learning. See http://www.muse-eek.com for details

Rhythms Volume 1
Spiral Bound ISBN 0-9648632-7-8   Perfect Bound ISBN 1890944-55-6

This 120 page book concentrates on eighth note rhythms and is a thesaurus of rhythmic patterns. All examples use one pitch, allowing the student to focus completely on time and rhythm. All exercises can be downloaded from the internet to facilitate learning.

Rhythms Volume 2
Spiral Bound ISBN 0-9648632-8-6   Perfect Bound ISBN 1890944-56-4

This volume concentrates on sixteenth note rhythms, and is a 108 page thesaurus of rhythmic patterns. All examples use one pitch, allowing the student to focus completely on time and rhythm. All exercises can be downloaded from the internet to facilitate learning.

Rhythms Volume 3
Spiral Bound ISBN 0-890944-04-1   Perfect Bound ISBN 1890944-57-2

This volume concentrates on thirty second note rhythms, and is a 102 page thesaurus of rhythmic patterns. All examples use one pitch, allowing the student to focus completely on time and rhythm. All exercises can be downloaded from the internet to facilitate learning.

Odd Meters Volume 1
Spiral Bound ISBN 0-9648632-9-4   Perfect Bound ISBN 1890944-58-0

This book applies both eighth and sixteenth note rhythms to odd meter combinations. All examples use one pitch, allowing the student to focus completely on time and rhythm. Exercises can be downloaded from the internet to facilitate learning. This 100 page book is an essential sight reading tool. See http://www.muse-eek.com for details.

Contemporary Rhythms Volume 1
Spiral Bound ISBN 1-890944-27-0   Perfect Bound ISBN 1890944-84-X

This volume concentrates on eight note rhythms and is a thesaurus of rhythmic patterns. Each exercise uses one pitch which allows the student to focus completely on time and rhythm. Exercises use modern innovations common to twentieth century notation, thereby familiarizing the student with the most sophisticated systems likely to be encountered in the course of a musical career. All exercises can be downloaded from the internet to facilitate learning.

Contemporary Rhythms Volume 2
Spiral Bound ISBN 1-890944-28-9   Perfect Bound ISBN 1890944-85-8

This volume concentrates on sixteenth note rhythms and is a thesaurus of rhythmic patterns. Each exercise uses one pitch which allows the student to focus completely on time and rhythm. Exercise use modern innovations common to twentieth century notation, thereby familiarizing the student with the most sophisticated systems likely to be encountered in the course of a musical career. All exercises can be downloaded from the internet to facilitate learning. See http://www.muse-eek.com for details.

Independence Volume 1
Spiral Bound ISBN 1-890944-00-9   Perfect Bound ISBN 1890944-83-1

This 51 page book is designed for pianists, stick and touchstyle guitarists, percussionists and anyone who wishes to develop the rhythmic independence of their hands. This volume concentrates on quarter, eighth and sixteenth note rhythms and is a thesaurus of rhythmic patterns. The exercises in this book gradually incorporate more and more complex rhythmic patterns making it an excellent tool for both the beginning and the advanced student.

Other Guitar Study Aids

Right Hand Technique for Guitar Volume 1
Spiral Bound ISBN 0-9648632-6-X   Perfect Bound ISBN 1890944-54-8

Here's a breakthrough in music instruction, using the internet as a teaching tool! This book gives a concise method for developing right hand technique on the guitar, one of the most overlooked and under-addressed aspects of learning the instrument. The simplest, most basic movements are used to build fatigue-free technique. Exercises can be downloaded from the internet to facilitate learning.

Single String Studies Volume One
Spiral Bound ISBN 1-890944-01-7   Perfect Bound ISBN 1890944-62-9

This book is an excellent learning tool for both the beginner who has no experience reading music on the guitar, and the advanced student looking to improve their ledger line reading and general knowledge of each string of the guitar. Each exercise concentrates the students attention on one string at a time. This allows a familiarity to form between the written pitch and where it can be found on the guitar along with improving one's "feel" for jumping linearly across the fretboard. Exercises can be downloaded from the internet to facilitate learning.

Single String Studies Volume Two
Spiral Bound ISBN 1-890944-05-X   Perfect Bound ISBN 1890944-64-5

This book is a continuation of Volume One, but using non-diatonic notes. Volume Two helps the intermediate and advanced student improve their ledger line reading and general knowledge of each string of the guitar. Exercises can be downloaded from the internet to facilitate learning.

Single String Studies for Bass Guitar Volume One
Spiral Bound ISBN 1-890944-02-5   Perfect Bound ISBN 1890944-63-7

This book is an excellent learning tool for both the beginner who has no experience reading music on the bass guitar, and the advanced student looking to improve their ledger line reading and general knowledge of each string of the bass. Each exercise concentrates a students attention of one string at a time. This allows a familiarity to form between the written pitch and where it can be found on the bass along with improving one's "feel" for jumping linearly across the fretboard. Exercises can be downloaded from the internet to facilitate learning.

Single String Studies for 5 String Bass Guitar Volume One
Spiral Bound ISBN 1-890944-95-5

This book is an excellent learning tool for both the beginner who has no experience reading music on the bass guitar, and the advanced student looking to improve their ledger line reading and general knowledge of each string of the bass. Each exercise concentrates a students attention of one string at a time. This allows a familiarity to form between the written pitch and where it can be found on the bass along with improving one's "feel" for jumping linearly across the fretboard. Exercises can be downloaded from the internet to facilitate learning.

Single String Studies for Bass Guitar Volume Two
Spiral Bound ISBN 1-890944-06-8   Perfect Bound ISBN 1890944-65-3

This book is a continuation of Volume One, but using non-diatonic notes. Volume Two helps the intermediate and advanced student improve their ledger line reading and general knowledge of each string of the bass. Each exercise concentrates the students attention on one string at a time. This allows a familiarity to form between the written pitch and where it can be found on the bass along with improving one's "feel" for jumping linearly across the fretboard. Exercises can be downloaded from the internet to facilitate learning.

Guitar Clinic
Spiral Bound ISBN 1-890944-45-9   Perfect Bound ISBN 1890944-86-6

Guitar Clinic" contains techniques and exercises Mr. Arnold uses in the clinics and workshops he teaches around the U.S.. Much of the material in this book is culled from Mr. Arnold's educational series, over thirty books in all. The student wishing to expand on his or her studies will find suggestions within the text as to which of Mr. Arnold's books will best serve their specific needs. Topics covered include: how to read music, sight reading, reading rhythms, music theory, chord and scale construction, modal sequencing, approach notes, reharmonization, bass and chord comping, and hexatonic scales.

The Essentials: Chord Charts, Scales, and Lead Patterns for the Guitar
Saddle Stitched (Stapled) ISBN 1-890944-94-7

This book is truly essential to the aspiring guitarist. It includes the most commonly played chords on the guitar in all keys, plus a bonus of the most commonly used scales and lead patterns. You can quickly learn all the chords, scales and lead patterns you need to know to play your favorite songs-and solo over them, too! "The Essentials" doesn't stop there, though. It also includes chord progressions to help you learn how to chord songs in folk, country, rock, blues and other popular styles. The books contain loads of easy to understand diagrams of chords, scales and lead patterns so you will be up and running in no time!

Sight Singing and Ear Training Series

The world is full of ear training and sight reading books, so why do we need more?
This sight singing and ear training series uses a different method of teaching relative pitch sight singing and ear training. The success of this method has been remarkable. Along with a new method of ear training these books also use CDs and the internet as a teaching tool! Audio files of all the exercises are easily downloaded from the internet at www.muse-eek.com By combining interactive audio files with a new approach to ear training a student's progress is limited only by their willingness to practice!

A Fanatic's Guide to Ear Training and Sight Singing
Spiral Bound ISBN 1-890944-19-X   Perfect Bound ISBN 1890944-75-0

This book and CD present a method for developing good pitch recognition through sight singing. This method differs from the myriad of other sight singing books in that it develops the ability to identify and name all twelve pitches within a key center. Through this method a student gains the ability to identify sound based on it's relationship to a key and not the relationship of one note to another (i.e. interval training as commonly taught in many texts). All note groupings from one to six notes are presented giving the student a thesaurus of basic note combinations which develops sight singing and note recognition to a level unattainable before this Guide's existence.

Key Note Recognition
Spiral Bound ISBN 1-890944-30-3   Perfect Bound ISBN 1890944-77-7

This book and CD present a method for developing the ability to recognize the function of any note against a key. This method is a must for anyone who wishes to sound one note on an instrument or voice and instantly know what key a song is in. Through this method a student gains the ability to identify a sound based on its relationship to a key and not the relationship of one note to another (i.e. interval training as commonly taught in many texts). Key Center Recognition is a definite requirement before proceeding to two note ear training.

LINES Volume One: Sight Reading and Sight Singing Exercises
Spiral Bound ISBN 1-890944-09-2   Perfect Bound ISBN 1890944-76-9

This book can be used for many applications. It is an excellent source for easy half note melodies that a beginner can use to learn how to read music or for sight singing slightly chromatic lines. An intermediate or advanced student will find exercises for multi-voice reading. These exercises can also be used for multi-voice ear training. The book has the added benefit in that all exercises can be heard by downloading the audio files for each example. See http://www.muse-eek.com for details.

Ear Training ONE NOTE: Beginning Level
Spiral Bound ISBN 1-890944-12-2   Perfect Bound ISBN 1890944-66-1

This Book and Audio CD presents a new and exciting method for developing relative pitch ear training. It has been used with great success and is now finally available on CD. There are three levels available depending on the student's ability. This beginning level is recommended for students who have little or no music training.

Ear Training ONE NOTE: Intermediate Level
Spiral Bound ISBN 1-890944-13-0   Perfect Bound ISBN 1890944-67-X

This Audio CD and booklet presents a new and exciting method of developing relative pitch ear training. It has been used with great success and is now finally available on CD. This intermediate level is recommended for students who have had some music training but still find their skills need more development.

Ear Training ONE NOTE: Advanced Level
Spiral Bound ISBN 1-890944-14-9   Perfect Bound ISBN 1890944-68-8

This Audio CD and booklet presents a new and exciting method of developing relative pitch ear training. It has been used with great success and is now finally available on CD. There are three levels available depending on the student's ability. This advanced level is recommended for students who have worked with the intermediate level and now wish to perfect their skills.   .

Ear Training TWO NOTE: Beginning Level Volume One
Spiral Bound ISBN 1-890944-31-9   Perfect Bound ISBN 1890944-69-6

This Book and Audio CD continues the method of developing relative pitch ear training as set forth in the "Ear Training, One Note" series. There are six volumes in the beginning level series. Through practice, the student eventually gains the ability to recognize the key and the names of any two notes played simultaneously. Volume One concentrates on 5ths. Prerequisite: a strong grasp of the One Note method.

Ear Training TWO NOTE: Beginning Level Volume Two
Spiral Bound ISBN 1-890944-32-7   Perfect Bound ISBN 1890944-70-X

This Book and Audio CD continues the method of developing relative pitch ear training as set forth in the "Ear Training, One Note" series. There are six volumes in the beginning level series. Through practice, the student eventually gains the ability to recognize the key and the names of any two notes played simultaneously. Volume Two concentrates on 3rds. Prerequisite: a strong grasp of the One Note method.

Ear Training TWO NOTE: Beginning Level Volume Three
Spiral Bound ISBN 1-890944-33-5   Perfect Bound ISBN 1890944-71-8

This Book and Audio CD continues the method of developing relative pitch ear training as set forth in the "Ear Training, One Note" series. There are six volumes in the beginning level series. Through practice, the student eventually gains the ability to recognize the key and the names of any two notes played simultaneously. Volume Three concentrates on 6ths. Prerequisite: a strong grasp of the One Note method.

Ear Training TWO NOTE: Beginning Level Volume Four
Spiral Bound ISBN 1-890944-34-3   Perfect Bound ISBN 1890944-72-6

This Book and Audio CD continues the method of developing relative pitch ear training as set forth in the "Ear Training, One Note" series. There are six volumes in the beginning level series. Through practice, the student eventually gains the ability to recognize the key and the names of any two notes played simultaneously. Volume Four concentrates on 4ths. Prerequisite: a strong grasp of the One Note method.

Ear Training TWO NOTE: Beginning Level Volume Five
Spiral Bound ISBN 1-890944-35-1   Perfect Bound ISBN 1890944-73-4

This Book and Audio CD continues the method of developing relative pitch ear training as set forth in the "Ear Training, One Note" series. There are six volumes in the beginning level series. Through practice, the student eventually gains the ability to recognize the key and the names of any two notes played simultaneously. Volume Five concentrates on 2nds. Prerequisite: a strong grasp of the One Note method.

Ear Training TWO NOTE: Beginning Level Volume Six
Spiral Bound ISBN 1-890944-36-X   Perfect Bound ISBN 1890944-74-2

This Book and Audio CD continues the method of developing relative pitch ear training as set forth in the "Ear Training, One Note" series. There are six volumes in the beginning level series. Through practice, the student eventually gains the ability to recognize the key and the names of any two notes played simultaneously. Volume Six concentrates on 7ths. Prerequisite: a strong grasp of the One Note method.

Comping Styles Series

This series is built on the progressions found in Chord Workbook Volume One. Each book covers a specific style of music and presents exercises to help a guitarist, bassist or drummer master that style. Audio CDs are also available so a student can play along with each example and really get "into the groove."

Comping Styles for the Guitar Volume Two FUNK
Spiral Bound ISBN 1-890944-07-6   Perfect Bound ISBN 1890944-60-2

This volume teaches a student how to play guitar or piano in a funk style. 36 Progressions are presented: 12 keys of a Major and Minor Blues plus 12 keys of Rhythm Changes A different groove is presented for each exercise giving the student a wide range of funk rhythms to master.   An Audio CD is also included so a student can play along with each example and really get "into the groove." The audio CD contains "trio" versions of each exercise with Guitar, Bass and Drums.

Comping Styles for the Bass Volume Two FUNK
Spiral Bound ISBN 1-890944-08-4   Perfect Bound ISBN 1890944-61-0

This volume teaches a student how to play bass in a funk style. 36 Progressions are presented: 12 keys of a Major and Minor Blues plus 12 keys of Rhythm Changes A different groove is presented for each exercise giving the student a wide range of funk rhythms to master.   An Audio CD is also included so a student can play along with each example and really get "into the groove." The audio CD contains "trio" versions of each exercise with Guitar, Bass and Drums.

Jazz and Blues Bass Line
Spiral Bound ISBN 1-890944-15-7   Perfect Bound ISBN 1890944-16-5

This book covers the basics of bass line construction. A theoretical guide to building bass lines is presented along with 36 chord progressions utilizing the twelve keys of a Major and Minor Blues, plus twelve keys of Rhythm Changes. A reharmonization section is also provided which demonstrates how to reharmonize a chord progression on the spot.

Time Series

The Doing Time series presents a method for contacting, developing and relying on your internal time sense: This series is an excellent source for any musician who is serious about developing strong internal sense of time. This is particularly useful in any kind of music where the rhythms and time signatures may be very complex or free, and there is no conductor.

THE BIG METRONOME
Spiral Bound ISBN 1-890944-37-8   Perfect Bound ISBN 1890944-82-3

The Big Metronome is designed to help you develop a better internal sense of time. This is accomplished by requiring you to "feel time" rather than having you rely on the steady click of a metronome. The idea is to slowly wean yourself away from an external device and rely on your internal/natural sense of time. The exercises presented work in conjunction with the three CDs that accompany this book. CD 1 presents the first 13 settings from a traditional metronome 40-66; the second CD contains metronome markings 69-116, and the third CD contains metronome markings 120-208. The first CD gives you a 2 bar count off and a click every measure, the second CD gives you a 2 bar count off and a click every 2 measures, the 3rd CD gives you a 2 bar count off and a click every 4 measures. By presenting all common metronome markings a student can use these 3 CDs as a replacement for a traditional metronome.

Doing Time with the Blues Volume One:
Spiral Bound ISBN 1-890944-17-3   Perfect Bound ISBN 1890944-78-5

The book and CD presents a method for gaining an internal sense of time thereby eliminating dependence on a metronome. The book presents the basic concept for developing good time and also includes exercises that can be practiced with the CD. The CD provides eight 8 minute tracks at different tempos in which the time is delineated every 2 bars, and with an extra hit every 12 bars to outline the blues form. The student may then use the exercises presented in the book to gain control of their execution or improvise to gain control of their ideas using this bare minimum of time delineation.

Doing Time with the Blues Volume Two:
Spiral Bound ISBN 1-890944-18-1   Perfect Bound ISBN 1890944-79-3

This is the 2nd volume of a four volume series which presents a method for developing a musician's internal sense of time, thereby eliminating dependence on a metronome. This 2nd volume presents different exercises which further the development of this time sense. This 2nd volume begins to test even a professional level player's ability. The CD provides eight 8 minute tracks at different tempos in which the time is delineated every 4 bars with an extra hit every 12 bars to outline the blues form. New exercises are also included that can be practiced with the CD. This series is an excellent source for any musician who is serious about developing an internal sense of time.

Doing Time with 32 bars Volume One:
Spiral Bound ISBN 1-890944-22-X   Perfect Bound ISBN Spiral Bound ISBN
1890944-80-7

The book and CD presents a method for gaining an internal sense of time thereby
eliminating dependence on a metronome. The book presents the basic concept for
developing good time and also includes exercises that can be practiced with the
CD. The CD provides eight 8 minute tracks at different tempos in which the time
is delineated every 2 bars, with an extra hit every 32 to outline the 32 bar form.
The student may then use the exercises presented in the book to gain control of
their execution or improvise to gain control of their ideas using this bare minimum
of time delineation.

Doing Time with 32 bars Volume Two:
Spiral Bound ISBN 1-890944-23-8   Perfect Bound ISBN Spiral Bound ISBN
1890944-81-5

This is the 2nd volume of a four volume series which presents a method for
developing a musician's internal sense of time, thereby eliminating dependence on
a metronome.. This 2nd volume presents different exercises which further the
development of this time sense. This 2nd volume begins to test even a professional level player's ability. The CD provides eight 8 minute tracks at different
tempos in which the time is delineated every 4 bars with an extra hit every 32 bars
to outline the 32 bar form.   New exercises are also included that can be practiced
with the CD. This series is an excellent source for any musician who is serious
about developing an internal sense of time.

Other Books

Music Theory Workbook for All Instruments, Volume 1: Interval and Chord Construction
Spiral Bound ISBN 1890944-92-0   Perfect Bound ISBN 1890944-46-7

This book provides real hands-on application of intervals and chords. A theory
section written in concise and easy to understand language prepares the student
for all exercises. Worksheets are given that quiz a student about intervals and
chord construction using staff notation. Answers are supplied in the back of the
book enabling a student to work without a teacher.

MY MUSIC: Explorations in the Application of 12 Tone Techniques to Jazz Composition and Improvisation
Spiral Bound ISBN 1890944-10-6

Bruce Arnold, the New York-based guitarist-composer, educator, and author, has
achieved a strikingly original sound by applying jazz improvisational techniques to
late 20th century 12-tone compositional methods. His live performances and
recordings with The Bruce Arnold Trio consist of adventurous explorations of this
unexpectedly combustible sonic combination. This book takes an in depth look at
the techniques he uses to derive his signature sound.

Full scores of all compositions are included in the book. The Paperback edition
contains an audio CD with all relevant compositions. The ebook edition supplies
links to an on-line archive of fully downloadable audio examples in mp3 format.

E-Books

The Bruce Arnold series of instructional E-books is for the student who wishes to target specific areas of study that are of particular interest. Many of these books are excerpted from other larger texts. The excerpted source is listed for each book. These books are available on-line at www.muse-eek.com as well as at many e-tailers throughout the internet.

Chord Velocity: Volume One, Learning to switch between chords quickly
E-book ISBN 1-890944-88-2

The first hurdle a beginning guitarist encounters is difficulty in switching between chords quickly enough to make a chord progression sound like music. This book provides exercises that help a student gradually increase the speed with which they change chords. Special free audio files are also available on the muse-eek.com website to make practice more productive and fun. With a few weeks, remarkable improvement by can be achieved using this method. This book is excerpted from "1st Steps for a Beginning Guitarist Volume One."

Guitar Technique: Volume One, Learning the basics to fast, clean, accurate and fluid performance skills.
E-book ISBN 1-890944-91-2

This book is for both the beginning guitarist or the more experienced guitarist who wishes to improve their technique. All aspects of the physical act of playing the guitar are covered, from how to hold a guitar to the specific way each hand is involved in the playing process. Pictures and videos are provided to help clarify each technique. These pictures and videos are either contained in the book or can be downloaded at www.muse-eek.com This book is excerpted from "1st Steps for a Beginning Guitarist Volume One."

Accompaniment: Volume One, Learning to Play Bass and Chords Simultaneously
E-book ISBN 1-890944-87-4

The techniques found within this book are an excellent resource for creating and understanding how to play bass and chords simultaneously in a jazz or blues style. Special attention is paid to understanding how this technique is created, thereby enabling the student to recreate this style with other pieces of music. This book is excerpted from the book "Guitar Clinic."

Beginning Rhythm Studies: Volume One, Learning the basics of reading rhythm and playing in time.
E-book ISBN 1-890944-89-0

This book covers the basics for anyone wishing to understand or improve their rhythmic abilities. Simple language is used to show the student how to read and play rhythm. Exercises are presented which can accelerate the learning process. Audio examples in the form of midifiles are available on the muse-eek.com website to facilitate learning the correct rhythm in time. This book is excerpted from the book "Rhythm Primer."

MY MUSIC: Explorations in the Application of 12 Tone Techniques to Jazz Composition and Improvisation
E-book ISBN 1890944-10-6

Bruce Arnold, the New York-based guitarist-composer, educator, and author, has achieved a strikingly original sound by applying jazz improvisational techniques to late 20th century 12-tone compositional methods. His live performances and recordings with The Bruce Arnold Trio consist of adventurous explorations of this unexpectedly combustible sonic combination. This book takes an in depth look at the techniques he uses to derive his signature sound. Full scores of all compositions are included in the book. The ebook edition supplies links to an on-line archive of fully downloadable audio examples in mp3 format.